Every Child An Achiever

A Parent's Guide to the Kumon Method

"There is no elevator to success;
you have to take the stairs."
— *posted on the wall of a Kumon Center*

The Kumon Math and Reading program is one of the most overlooked success stories in education.

– Ron Sheehy, Ph.D., father, Research Associate,
The Andrew Young School of Policy Studies,
Georgia State University, Atlanta, Georgia

We have found Kumon to be an outstanding method of individualizing for various abilities in students. Every student can be working at a level that is challenging. No student has to wait for others to catch up. Students move at their own pace. Kumon teaches focus, concentration and the ability to work hard.

– Patricia Hollingsworth, Ph.D., Director,
The University School, Tulsa, OK

My wife and I like the Kumon strategy and the discipline of working daily to build skills and master subjects. We think Kumon's philosophy of 10 to 20 minutes a day of focused work is great. We think that Kumon is an excellent program in that it fosters the habit of work. It's a logical, well thought-out progression of work. We like it because it habituates [our son] to work challenges and master levels of work and then go on to the next level. . . . We're high on it. . . . We've brought a lot of our friends and their children to Kumon.

– Sandy Kress, father, Austin, TX,
former Senior Advisor to the President for Education Policy

My next-door neighbor has two children, and they came over one day and brought their Kumon homework. I watched these two–they were 6 and 4 at the time—and I was amazed at what I saw. These two children just sat at my kitchen table and whipped through their worksheets. Page after page. They had each been in Kumon about one year. I mean, it really stopped me in my tracks. At that point my little guy was just turning 4. I went to my neighbor and said, "What is this?!?" She explained Kumon, and I said, "Where do I sign?"

Now he is 5, and he sits at my kitchen table and he whips through his homework just like his friends do. I love the program. There are a lot of other things I would omit from my life before I would cut Kumon. Let's face it, I would never cut Kumon. I just

think to myself, if I had to take something away, it wouldn't be this.
— Bonnie Farias, mother, Danville, CA

One of the things I liked was that Kumon gives children work to do over the summer. I always thought that summer was such a dead time. I remember having 3 months off in the summer, then going back to school and spending 3 months repeating what we had done at the end of the last term. It was amazing how much I forgot over the summer. Now I think my children are always progressing 6 months ahead of any other child because they don't do all that relearning and rethinking.
— Jamie Pierce, mother, Unionville, ON

My daughter's math grades are just off the charts... I don't know what I would have done without Kumon. It should be in every school. I wish someone had told us about it earlier.
— Cindy Osterhout, mother, Seattle, WA

It's never a fight for Isabelle to come to Kumon because this is a social event for her. Sometimes she wants to do all her homework packets at once. "I want to do them all!" she says, and I have to slow her down.
— Tara Hogan, mother, Kirkwood, MO

Before we knew about Kumon, she was falling deeper and deeper through the cracks. Then I saw a Kumon poster and everything changed. She went from the bottom of her class to the top.
— Maria Gibb, mother, Saskatoon, SK

In our state, the educational system always seems to be experimenting with things; they always want to try something different. Every few years they say, "Let's do math this way," or "This approach isn't working, let's try something else." I don't worry about it much any more. I know our daughter is going to be OK because of what she's done in Kumon.
— Laura Henry, mother, Sacramento, CA

Every Child An Achiever
A Parent's Guide to the Kumon Method

Kumon North America, Inc.
Glenpointe Centre East
300 Frank W. Burr Boulevard, 5th floor
Teaneck, NJ 07666
201-928-0444

ISBN 0-9702092-2-3

Cover design by Nanette Hoey, Kumon

Book design, composition and printing by
Harmony Printing Limited
Toronto, Ontario, Canada

Table of Contents

Acknowledgements

It would be impossible to recognize all of the patient and supportive individuals who contributed to the creation of this book. The author and Kumon North America gratefully acknowledge the contributions of the many parents, students, Instructors and staff throughout Canada, the United States and Mexico with whom we met and spoke. We would especially like to thank:

The South Lake, TX, and Voorhees, NJ, Kumon Math and Reading Centers for allowing us to photograph their Centers "in action."

Matt Lupsha, Mary Mokris, Doreen Lawrence, Lisa Kaul, Mary Thurmond and Hiroaki Nihongi for their meticulous editing of the manuscript.

Nanette Hoey for design and graphics.

Kumon at a Glance

- **Kumon is the world's largest supplemental education program.** Over 3 million students are studying at 24,000 Kumon Centers in 44 countries around the world. There are about 150,000 students and 1,800 Centers in North America. These numbers are growing rapidly.

- Kumon has two programs: one for mastering math (from counting to calculus), and one for reading comprehension (from learning ABCs to making summaries and critical analyses of literature).

- Kumon provides a proven, time-tested system of learning for students of *all ages and skill levels,* whether they are average, gifted, or need remedial assistance. Many learning impaired students have also benefited from Kumon. Every type of student can benefit from Kumon.

- *Kumon begins from a philosophy.* Kumon believes that all children have enormous, unseen, untapped potential to learn and to grow. The goal of the Kumon Method is to provide each child with the tools, plan and guidance to achieve his or her full potential.

- Kumon is a highly *individualized* program. Different students naturally absorb knowledge at different rates; Kumon allows them to progress at their own pace. Students advance based on *individual ability* rather than age or grade.

- Kumon's individualized approach allows students to

achieve individual goals. Some enroll to "catch up," while others seek to move beyond their grade level at school.

- Kumon not only builds academic skills, but also strengthens *study habits*, improves *concentration* and increases *self-confidence* through its daily study program.

- By analyzing the records of millions of students over the past 50 years, Kumon has found that, on average, a student who does his or her work conscientiously for about 15-20 minutes a day for 9-12 months will show significant improvement. Kumon is not a "quick fix" or a cram course to prepare for an exam. With an investment of time and effort, Kumon begins to prove its value, and results improve from there on.

APPROACH

- Kumon is based on a simple concept: *practice makes perfect*. Both the math and reading programs progress in a linear fashion, advancing through a carefully planned series of very small incremental steps. Each step involves considerable practice.

- Through this repeated practice, students *master* skills before moving on. Each new concept builds on the foundation established by the previous one, and new exercises constantly review and strengthen previously learned skills.

- Since one goal of the Kumon Method is to make high school study easy, Kumon students are encouraged to reach an *advanced level of study*.

- The key to Kumon is to start the child at a *comfortable starting point*, where he or she can consistently solve 100% of the problems in a given amount of time. This increases self-confidence and allows the student to experience success right from the start.

PRACTICE

- Students visit a Kumon Center twice a week to study under the guidance of a certified Kumon Instructor. They stay for about half an hour per subject.

- Students do *homework* on all non-Center days. Children are expected to work daily, with parental support and assistance. The parents' role is praising and motivating their child to maintain this daily study habit and is absolutely essential.

- Kumon is designed not to be a burden to either parent or child—homework for either the math or reading program will take most children about 15-20 minutes per subject.

For more information, call 1-800-ABC-MATH, or log onto www.kumon.com for information and to locate the nearest Kumon Center.

Preface

Back in 1992, I began to research a "new" educational program that was making headlines across the United States. A system of learning called Kumon was attracting attention because it focused on building basic skills through repetition and daily homework, and because Kumon students were showing dramatically improved test scores, publications such as *TIME*, *Newsweek*, *The Wall Street Journal* and others were quick to pick up on this phenomenon. Writers just like me were startled to see young children doing advanced math problems, and even children with learning disabilities developing the ability to study beyond their normal school grade level instead of years behind it.

I traveled all over North America researching that book. I interviewed Kumon Instructors, parents and children in the U.S. and Canada. In particular, listening to mothers and fathers talk about Kumon and the changes they saw in their children as a result of Kumon study began to erode my journalistic objectivity, and I soon found myself looking at Kumon just as any other parent would. I had questions and doubts and even misgivings about the Kumon system, and I voiced those to Instructors and Kumon staff alike. Everyone answered my questions directly and persuasively. That, combined with what I saw day after day in my visits to Kumon Math and Reading Centers, convinced me of the effectiveness of the Kumon Method and the tremendous results it can produce.

Of course, I was not supposed to be writing an advertisement for Kumon. I was supposed to find out what *TIME* and *Newsweek* were talking about, summarize it, and put it into language that the average parent could understand. I was a hard-nosed journalist accustomed to publishing in no-nonsense, button-down publications such as *The Harvard Business Review* and *Business Library Journal*. And yet, in the course of just a few weeks I was completely won over by what I saw and heard in Kumon Centers. I explained my findings to my wife, and we decided to try Kumon for ourselves (suffice it to say that our son showed significant progress within one year of enrollment, and both my wife and I have been very pleased). My work culminated in a brief introduction to the Kumon Method called *Every Child an Achiever* (published by Intercultural Group, New York, 1993).

Fast-forward almost a decade. One day someone in the U.S. wrote to me about *Every Child an Achiever*. The only topic I had talked about in that book was the Kumon Math program. "What about the reading program?" this person asked. Why had I ignored it?

The answer was simple: at the time I wrote that book nearly ten years ago, there was no Kumon Reading program to speak of. I wrote back to explain that reading comprehension seemed to be a big part of Kumon these days but that frankly I was out of touch.

This one letter and my response to it started me thinking. It wasn't just that I was out of touch: *Every Child an Achiever* was out of date. After some more consideration, I suggested to Kumon that perhaps it was time to update the old book. I knew that any good publisher would be interested in backing the project, but it was also necessary to get assistance from Kumon's North American headquarters in New Jersey to help arrange interviews and highlight some of the key changes in the program over the past decade.

They liked the idea, and also said it would be good to look at Kumon once again with a parent's eyes and tell the story that way rather than having some Kumon executive explain it. In just a couple of weeks I was back on the road, camera and tape recorder in hand just like the old days, talking to Kumon parents and children.

*   *   *

This book is the result of that research. I traveled from New York to Honolulu, Tulsa to Toronto, Miami to Seattle, and a dozen cities in between. I met with hundreds of people and listened to them tell me about their children, their students, their parents, and their experiences with Kumon. I have tried to summarize what they told me in these pages.

As you read, you will undoubtedly have questions. That is natural. I have tried to anticipate as many of those questions as possible. But no book can answer all your questions. My advice: Go to find your local Kumon Center and talk to an Instructor. If you can't find a Kumon Center near your home or would just like to talk to someone about Kumon, check out www.kumon.com on the Internet, or look at the list of Contact Information at the back of this book. (Feel free to stop your reading at any point and go looking for answers to your questions via the telephone or the Internet.) When you are finished, come back to the text and read on. The more you know about Kumon, the better you can make an informed decision about what is best for your child.

One last note: Although the material contained herein applies to anyone interested in Kumon in any part of the world, this book is intended for parents in North America, so all the geographic and cultural references are specific to that region.

I hope all your kids learn, as mine did, that taking the stairs may seem more challenging at first, but it's a lot more rewarding in the end.

David W. Russell
September 2002

One Mom's Tale

Kumon Makes All the Difference

Not long ago I met an inspirational woman in Seattle, named Jeannie Iannelli. When I asked her how she became involved with Kumon, she told me this story. I know she would not mind if I shared it with you.

> It was in the spring of my son Jamie's 4th grade year. It was late at night on a school night. I heard crying coming from his room so I went upstairs to see what was the matter. I said, "Honey, what's wrong?" and he answered, "Why am I so stupid? What's wrong with me? I'm the only one in the class that doesn't get fractions. I hate myself! Why did God make me so stupid?!"

> Needless to say, I was extremely concerned. I spoke with his teacher the next day about this. And do you know what the teacher said to me? "Don't worry, he'll catch up."

> That's when I knew we were in trouble. I went to the local academic aids store and bought math workbooks. I made Jamie do an hour a night of math. He hated it and me, and I didn't know what I was doing. I just knew I was desperate to help him.

A while later I was talking to a neighbor about Jamie's struggles in math. She told me that her son, who was Jamie's age, did "Kumon." I had never heard of it, but I went with her the next week to meet the Instructor. Jamie started at Level 4A, a very basic level, far below the capabilities of an average 4th grader. I was alarmed at how easy the Kumon work was for him at the beginning, but I was desperate and willing to give Kumon a chance.

To make a long story short, by the time Jamie was in the 6th grade he tested into the honors math program. From then on he got an A in math in every class all the way through high school, including AP calculus, and was always in the honors classes.

I shudder to think what would have happened if we hadn't found Kumon when we did. I really believe that it saved Jamie. It made all the difference in his self-confidence and his vision of himself as a strong and capable student. If we hadn't found Kumon, it is entirely possible that Jamie's lack of self-confidence in math would have manifested itself in other subjects in middle school, which is such a crucial time for students.

Jamie graduated from high school last spring and now attends Loyola University in New Orleans. We would have had a hard time sending him to such a good college out of state, but once again his academic achievements paid off—he was awarded a merit scholarship. Truly, Kumon has made all the difference for my son.

You probably won't be too surprised to hear that Jamie's mom became a Kumon Instructor. Now she says,

When parents ask me if Kumon really works, I always say 'Yes, absolutely,' and I tell them I have proof. Then I tell them the story of my son, Jamie. He's Exhibit A for me. If they are interested in hearing more, there are lots of parents here with similar stories, some of them even more dramatic. But I always start with my own child, because that's what got me hooked on Kumon."

Introduction

Why Consider Kumon?

There are many good reasons to consider Kumon for your children, regardless of their current performance in school. Kumon helps all children—average students, overachievers, those in need of remedial work, children with learning disabilities, students with limited proficiency in English—virtually anyone. Kumon is designed to help any child progress from whatever his or her current level may be to a much higher level of study, and to do so *with absolute mastery of the material.* The latter is something that even good grades in school cannot guarantee. In short, for students who are already doing well in school, Kumon offers far greater opportunities to develop their potential to its fullest. It's like opening a door for your children to enter a world of learning with nothing to hold them back. For children who are not doing as well in school, Kumon offers the opportunity to catch up to grade level and to then move ahead of it.

As a prologue to that explanation, let me give you three important reasons that leap immediately to my mind.

You should consider Kumon for your children if you sincerely want to:

- Guarantee that they have a strong academic foundation
- Build lifelong study habits, self-confidence and self-esteem

- Lessen the anxiety associated with schoolwork
  Let's take a quick look at these points.

By enrolling in Kumon, parents assure that their children will acquire a *strong academic foundation.* Kumon does not teach the basics of every academic discipline, only math and reading, because these are the twin cornerstones of all other learning. Children who master math and reading skills from an early age generally have an easier time with school. Whatever courses your children may take—history, science, social studies, etc.—the solid foundation they get in Kumon will help them to succeed in every area. In many cases, children not only keep up with their school class, but in a fairly short time progress to study beyond their school grade level.

Children who study Kumon also develop a lifelong *study habit.* They acquire the skills and attitudes necessary to grow into diligent students and responsible adults. They learn *self-discipline,* which will be essential to succeeding in any other endeavor they undertake for the rest of their lives. Kumon trains children to study on their own, to solve problems and progress through higher levels of learning, which leads to a new sense of *self-esteem.* As they discover the rewards of working for 100% mastery of each step in a particular subject, they develop a special sense of *self-confidence.* All of these qualities have a major impact on a child's emotional growth and sense of well-being, which go far beyond helping them to get good grades.

Kumon provides a systematic approach that starts where children's needs are and helps instill confidence, which translates into emotional adjustment over many areas. The confidence that Kumon instills in children crosses over [into] their lives in other areas which helps them to be successful.

**– Roy Walsh, Executive Director,
Children's Aid Society of Halton, ON**

Another feature of Kumon that is often overlooked is that it helps children to *lessen anxieties* associated with school work, both now and in the future. Children who do Kumon tend to find academic work in most subjects (not just math and reading) much less intimidating than their peers. Kumon teaches children the most important foundation of academics, and it teaches them more: how to study, how to solve problems, and how to reveal newfound knowledge in test-taking situations. All these things contribute to increased knowledge as well as increased self-confidence in school, and that combination translates into decreasing anxiety.

Of course, there is no guarantee that any child will like school or make friends or be successful. But children who do Kumon report again and again that school work is "not threatening," a surprising number say school is "easy." The earlier children gain this feeling of security in their own abilities, the more years they have to enjoy all the good things that school environments provide. Children who spend less time worrying about homework in junior high or high school have a lot more time to enjoy sports, music, drama, art, and all the other worthwhile attractions their world has to offer.

Testing is Unavoidable; Test-related Stress is Very Avoidable

One particular kind of childhood anxiety that we hear a lot about these days is sometimes called "math phobia." Many parents say they had it themselves and that's one reason they want their children to do Kumon. "I never got a 'math gene,'" said one mother, "and I want to make sure that my children don't have to go through the struggles I did with math. That's why they're in Kumon."

Later on, in Chapter 6, we will hear William J. Bennett and the co-authors of *The Educated Child* explain that,

> 'Math anxiety' arises from not being able to work problems correctly, not understanding important concepts, and not being able to get the right answer when it's your turn at the blackboard. The antidote to such anxiety is greater familiarity with math. And such familiarity comes through repeated exposure. There is no better way for children to gain confidence about working problems and tackling challenges.
>
> (Reprinted with the permission of The Free Press, a Division of Simon & Schuster Adult Publishing Group,

In other words, repeated practice is the best way to eliminate these anxieties. The Kumon Method approaches any subject, and especially math, from just this perspective: to provide a child with lots of problems and constant repetition, all aimed at attaining mastery of the material. It is no surprise, then, that Kumon students never seem the slightest bit concerned about any kind of "math fear."

There is another anxiety spreading throughout our schools, one much more pervasive than math fear. It has to do with students being given standardized tests, a sharpened pencil, and a strict time limit in which to demonstrate their total knowledge of a subject. The results of these exams are being increasingly used to judge who will advance to what academic program within a school, which will get into what university, and even which schools will get federal funding and which will not.

When you and I went to school there were already plenty of tests—not only in our regular classes, but also various kinds of achievement tests, personality tests, and college entrance tests (either the SATs or ACTs). Many of us didn't pay much attention to them because any test that didn't directly affect your grade in a particular course didn't really matter. Children today have even more tests to take. Competition is tougher, and applicant profiles at most universities are far more diverse than they used to be. Many feel that the only way to judge children from widely differing backgrounds is to see how well they do on standardized tests.

In the United States, testing has become institutionalized for all students, right down to the elementary school level. In January 2002, President Bush signed HR1, the Congressional reauthorization of the Elementary and Secondary Education Act (ESEA), which is the major federal funding mandate for public schools. This revised Act, known as "No Child Left Behind," aims to foster and measure improvements in U.S. public school education. The measurement will be done by widespread testing. By 2005, states must annually administer standardized math and reading tests for all public school students in grades 3-8. (Incidentally, this same legislation allows qualified students attending "failing" schools to use public funds for supplemental education services. As of this writing, Kumon has been officially approved as a provider of supplemental education services in many states.)

For many children today, test-taking is an increasing source of anxiety. Parents report that timed tests in particular are a source of stress, and virtually all standardized tests these days are timed. This is one area where Kumon students have a big advantage over other children. Kumon students practice math and reading every single day, and they are trained to time their daily assignments not only in the Kumon Center but for homework as well. It does not put extra pressure on students; in fact, just the opposite. Children quickly become accustomed to timing themselves (this is very different from "working against the clock" as a group in a high-pressure, classroom setting).

Our daughter did very well on her IQ tests in kindergarten. We know that Kumon doesn't build IQ, but we believe that because she learned how to display her innate ability thanks to Kumon, she may have tested better than other children.

– Hanif Rajpurkar, father, Maryland Heights, MO

Winning Formula: School + Kumon = Success

Where do we as sincere, concerned parents find ourselves today? We all seem to be busier than we ever imagined we would be, and it is frighteningly easy to convince ourselves that we are too busy to take an active role in our children's education. The simple solution that most of us opt for is to "outsource" the responsibility for education to our schools, both public and private. After all, that's what schools are there for, right? Aren't the tax dollars or tuition that we pay adequate assurance that our children are being educated?

Unfortunately, the further our children go in the educational system, the more difficult the competition is likely to get, and the more preparation they will need to meet it.

It is no surprise, then, that increasing numbers of parents are: 1) supplementing what is going on in school by sending our children to private educational programs, and 2) taking a few minutes every day from our busy schedules to make sure that we have some input into our children's education. In other words, parents today are feeling a greater responsibility to *do something* about the quality of their children's education.

They are people just like you and me who want their children to have a chance to do well in school without struggle or strain, and have a good chance to get into the university of their choice. These are normal parents who want what every parent wants: for their children to be happy, to lead successful lives both in school and beyond which is why, year after year, tens of thousands of parents choose Kumon.

Chapter 1

What is Kumon?

Upon hearing the name, perhaps from a friend, a teacher or in a newspaper or magazine story, every parent's first question is, "What exactly *is* Kumon?" It's a simple question, and it deserves a simple, clear answer. However, to answer that question properly requires a brief explanation about Kumon's history, philosophy and methodology, all of which could fill more space than we have room for in this book. Instead, let's keep it simple. Here are 10 keys to understanding Kumon:

1) **Kumon is a supplemental system of education.** "Supplemental" means that it is not designed as a substitute for school-based learning. It adds to regular school studies, and in fact it was designed to make school much easier. School is meant to be the foundation of a child's education. In theory, it is the place where a child develops his or her mind, body and character. School is a place to study academic subjects, as well as to develop study skills and social skills.

Parents decide to come to Kumon because they want something more for their children than what their local school system can offer. Kumon provides a strong, well-structured supplemental system of learning, with regular homework and parental involvement.

Parents faced with similar situations and looking for a home-based supplement to regular school may decide to hire a tutor. However, many parents complain that the "ideal" of tutoring is very far from the reality. To borrow the words of one mother in Miami, "A tutor is just someone you hire to provide information. He doesn't really know your child, doesn't care about her progress; he's just getting paid to offer up his knowledge. And tutors have no set method. They jump around from one thing to another and there's no guarantee that your child is getting all the basics and also advancing. With Kumon you never have to worry about that."

Kumon provides a carefully structured approach to learning specific subjects. Students advance at their own pace through higher and higher levels. Where a tutor spoon-feeds a child with information, Kumon allows the child to learn on his or her own, though still within a fixed framework of knowledge.

In short, Kumon is a structured supplement to regular schoolwork. It is designed for parents who want to be certain that their children have the maximum chance to develop their potential as learners, regardless of age or ability.

My daughter was slipping between the cracks. We went through a lot of tutors for three years from third grade on. Her teachers were very worried. We had to play catch-up. Then she enrolled in the Kumon Reading program and the Math program. Now she tells people "I only get A's," and it's true! She's a straight-A student.

– Cindy Osterhout, mother, Seattle, WA

---

2) **Kumon was started by a concerned parent.** Kumon was created almost 50 years ago by a Japanese math teacher named Toru Kumon who wanted to help his son do better in school. Mr. Kumon was just a concerned parent who was not satisfied with the way his child was learning. He created a simple, step-by-step system to teach young children the subject he knew best: mathematics. In time it developed into the Kumon Method, and into a global business. Mr. Kumon realized that his system could be used for anyone, not just children

(I recently talked to a 60-year-old man in California who is studying Kumon) and for almost any subject.

Toru Kumon passed away in 1995, but his son Hiroshi now carries on his great legacy. And that legacy has grown far beyond its humble beginnings, spanning the globe and gathering millions of students, teaching them in different languages and responding to their needs in different countries.

Searching for the real potential of children is the aim of good education.

– Toru Kumon

---

3) **Kumon develops three different kinds of skills for success:**

a) *Academic skills:* Kumon is best known for its ability to build academic knowledge and boost academic achievement. Specifically, the system is designed to improve knowledge and understanding in two basic areas, mathematics and reading comprehension. Kumon considers math and reading to be the most critical for any student who hopes to advance through junior high and high school and then on to college.

Kumon prepares students to handle college-level mathematics with ease and to be able to read, understand, and critique English prose. These are exactly the academic skills that students need to enter and to succeed in good universities and to function in our society.

You might be surprised to hear that some people at MIT are struggling with math, but it happens. I see some kids in my dorm staying up all night trying to get their homework done. Not me. Kumon gave me a stong math background so that I didn't struggle with my homework like some of my peers.

– Frederick Wang, former Kumon student, now an undergraduate, Massachusetts Institute of Technology

---

b) *Study skills:* Kumon improves study skills dramatically. Kumon students do brief homework assignments every day. No vacations, no holidays. Homework time is kept short to make it easier for students to maintain this commitment, but it is essential that children do Kumon every day. By insisting on daily study, keeping the assignments manageable, then rewarding success through Instructor praise, Kumon motivates students to build and maintain lifelong study habits.

Kumon sure made math courses in high school easy. Now, in college, I'm usually finished with studying by 9 or 10 PM, way earlier than the other guys I know.

– Nilsson Kocher, former Kumon student, now an undergraduate, Harvard University

---

c) ***Test-taking skills:*** Kumon prepares students to perform well on tests, not only by having a solid academic foundation, but by learning how to solve problems quickly and accurately. When a student can think clearly, arrive at a correct answer quickly, and move on to more difficult parts of a test without worrying about how much time is left, that child is very likely to outperform his or her peers. In Kumon, all work is timed: homework, class work, placement and achievement tests, and so on. Any child who is used to doing Kumon assumes that all tests are timed and doesn't think twice about it.

. . . You go to school, and it takes everyone an hour to do a test, and you're done in 10 minutes...

– Allison Friedman, Kumon student, Toronto, ON

Timed tests? They're not a problem. We are used to being timed. We usually finish early and have lots of extra time to go back and look for careless errors and that transfers to other subjects as well.

– Steve Chu, 16, one of three siblings doing Kumon in Sacramento, CA,

---

4) **Kumon is a highly individualized system that emphasizes self-learning.** An easy way to visualize Kumon is to think of it as a narrow path up a steep mountain. Rather than a rugged, arduous climb, the Kumon path consists of thousands of short, evenly spaced steps. Every child proceeds along the exact same path, completing worksheets in sequence. However, each child starts at a different point on that path, and each child proceeds at the pace that is most appropriate

for his or her individual abilities. No one loses their footing because they started too far ahead or missed some small part of the material that came before.

The important point is that this process is *student-driven*, not pre-determined by some textbook, school curriculum or government mandate. Kumon effectively puts learning in the student's own hands. No one pushes a slow student to move ahead faster and no one holds a gifted student back. Each student advances when he or she is ready, no sooner and no later. Students feel liberated because they can move at their own pace and are in control of their own success.

I think school is aimed at the middle level of children. Children who are above the middle level or below it are going to suffer. Kumon is different; it lets children move at their own pace. I really like that.

– Nancy Kolker, mother, Tulsa, OK

---

5) **Kumon emphasizes mastery of the subject material.** One distinctive feature of Kumon is that in order for a student to advance by even a small "step" on this slope, all work must be 100% correct and it must be completed within a specific time range. This emphasis, not just on learning but on mastery, is central to the Kumon Method. You don't learn subtraction until you know addition. You don't learn to add 2-digit numbers until you can add 1-digit numbers quickly and accurately.

Kumon measures mastery by two means, *speed* and *accuracy*. Accuracy is easy to understand: either a worksheet is 100% correct or it isn't. If it isn't, there is room for improvement. Kumon insists on 100% accuracy in all things, and children very quickly learn to do the same. Speed is just as simple, but not as easy for parents to grasp right away. In effect, the completion time ranges established for all Kumon materials are a means to gauge a child's ability to concentrate on work as well as to retain knowledge. Younger children need to learn to focus and concentrate in order to succeed in school, and even more so in Kumon. Older children may have learned to concentrate, but if they cannot produce a correct answer within a reasonable amount of time, there is no way to say they have mastered the material. Kumon believes that learning is a process of building upon prior knowledge, not racing to reach some goal marker along the way.

6) **Kumon requires a serious effort by parents, too.** Kumon offers parents the opportunity to participate in the growth of their children's math and reading skills because they understand that education works best when mom and dad are involved.

If you think you can just drop your children off at some learning center and leave it up to someone else to make sure they are learning and progressing as they should, you had better look somewhere else. Kumon requires parents to get involved with their children's education. You have to make sure your child does his or her homework every day, and then you may have to grade the homework and see that corrections are made. In most cases, Kumon takes about 15-20 minutes a day. If your child's future success is worth taking 15-20 minutes a day from your busy schedule, you are ready to go talk to a Kumon Instructor.

7) **Kumon is a bit old-fashioned.** As a formalized method for learning, Kumon was developed about half a century ago, which means it pre-dates personal computers, calculators, and many of the education fads that have come and gone. Even today, in the high-tech 21st century, Kumon's basic tools for learning are still a pencil, an eraser, and printed exercises on paper.

As a mother in California said to me, "Kumon is something my grandmother would have related to. Pencil, paper and lots of practice until you get it right." This basic approach, relying on the content of the education rather than high-tech tools, is typical of Kumon.

8) **Kumon is also very up-to-date**. Even though it believes that the printed materials are the best way for students to learn, Kumon is not anti-technology. The company uses state-of-the-art information technology to help its growing network of Instructors stay informed, share ideas, track student progress and to streamline administrative procedures.

It has placed a large body of information about Kumon on the Internet (www.kumon.com).

Kumon's long history has the important advantage of providing a vast reservoir of data, covering millions of students worldwide that can be reviewed and analyzed for possible improvements to its math and reading materials. Every year, Kumon staff re-examine the program and fine-tune the teaching materials, looking for places to improve even one worksheet in a system of thousands so that children derive the maximum benefit from the program.

9) **Kumon is much more than a teaching method.** The Kumon system is much more than just pencils, worksheets and repetition. These are only tools to help achieve the limitless potential within each child.

Although millions of students have proved that diligent use of the Kumon Method is demonstrably effective at teaching math and reading, the ultimate purpose of Mr. Kumon's method is not to develop superior academic skills. The real goal of the Kumon Method is to provide an effective means to develop the untapped potential of each and every child.

In many ways, Toru Kumon was more of a philosopher than a mathematician. He was a devout believer in the potential of children. Not just gifted children, but underprivileged children, physically handicapped children, children with learning disabilities—virtually any child. Thus, when he spoke about education he very seldom talked specifically about math. Instead, he talked about children and the tremendous potential of young minds to absorb, to understand, and to skillfully make use of complex information.

Simply put, the Kumon Method is rooted in a belief that children are even more special than we imagine. Every Kumon Instructor believes in this philosophy, whether they articulate it or not. They all subscribe to Toru Kumon's fundamental idea that if you stimulate a child's mind, anything is possible.

It is our wish that as many children as possible have the opportunity to develop their potential. . . . We want to see all children grow to the limit of their capabilities. . . . We consider our mission to be the expansion of the potential of each and every child to the maximum degree. Through this dedication to education, we hope to contribute to the progress of humankind.

– Toru Kumon

---

10) **Kumon works.** There isn't any other way to say it. I have traveled all over North America and talked to countless Kumon parents. Regardless of income, social background, race, language, or any other factor, parents say the same thing over and over again: Kumon works. Even parents of handicapped children, parents of children with every kind of learning disability, Down's syndrome, autism, you name it, all tell me the same thing: we are seeing changes in our child that we never believed were possible.

I put it this way: Kumon helps to turn ordinary parents into believers, people who accept the fact that their children have more potential for greatness than they had ever imagined. But a happy mother in St. Louis put it much better: "Kumon is truly amazing. When I look at my son today, I think it's a miracle."

Chapter 2

Toru Kumon and the Beginnings of the Kumon Method

Toru Kumon admits that he was a lazy, good-for-nothing student when he was young. "My favorite activity was lying around the house," he later remarked of his boyhood in Kochi in the early 1920s. But at the age of 12 he was thrust into a new private school, one dedicated to a principle called *jigaku-jishuu* ("self-study, self-learning"). In his new math class, for example, the teacher did not stand at the blackboard and lecture, as did all other teachers Toru Kumon had known. Instead, the teacher told the students to work on their own at their desks, going through the prescribed textbook at whatever pace felt comfortable. If they had a question about anything they read, they could ask the teacher and get a clear explanation. Toru Kumon took to this system like a fish to water: "It suited me perfectly. I didn't want to be a great math student, but I did want to get far enough ahead so that I could take it easy. Also, I hated having teachers breathing down my neck, telling me what to do and giving lectures all the time."

Under this new, self-motivated system, Toru Kumon

progressed rapidly. When he reached equations on his own he thought, "Hey, this is fun. Why didn't they teach interesting stuff like this while we were in elementary school?" He zipped through the work and finished his junior high math program a year early. When he had to go to a regular high school afterwards, it felt like a giant step backwards. He looked around at the other students in his class. There were a few bright ones who followed the teacher's lessons perfectly. Then there was a large bunch in the middle who sort of understood what was going on but never really felt they were on solid ground because the class kept moving along so fast. Then there was a small group at the other end of the spectrum who always seemed to be lost, just struggling to keep up day to day. How inefficient, he thought, and what a waste of time and effort for the majority of children who need more time to really understand the textbook, and what a drag on the more advanced students who have to keep from getting too far ahead and losing the rest of the class.

Toru Kumon went on to study math at a nationally famous university and became a math teacher in public high schools afterwards. But he could never forget his days of "self-study, self-learning" in that private junior high, and came to the conclusion that regular schools were sadly inefficient. Worse yet, what they were wasting wasn't simply time, but the learning power of all the young minds that passed through their doors. But what could one teacher do to change an entire nationwide system? Toru Kumon simply did his best to work within the system and to teach his students that mathematics can be interesting.

Years passed, and he continued to teach in the public schools. Then one day something happened that changed the course of his life. Kumon told the story this way:

It all started with a test paper.

One day my wife came into my study carrying a sheet of paper. It was a math test that my son Takeshi (who was then in second grade) had taken. He had received a poor mark, which was unusual for him, but I didn't think anything of it. However, my wife seemed quite concerned.

'Is it all right to let him get marks like this? Don't you think we should teach him at home?' she asked with a worried tone.

At the time, I had been teaching high school math for 20 years, and frankly, it had never occurred to me to teach my own son math from the time he was in elementary school. What was the point?

'One bad mark is nothing to panic over. In the first place, I have no idea what or how to teach an elementary school child. As soon as he gets to junior high school I'll start teaching him a few things,' I answered, hoping to persuade her not to make such a fuss.

But my wife would not accept this. 'Can you guarantee that he'll be all right if you wait until he gets to junior high school?' she asked, and I didn't know what to answer. She went on, 'You love teaching other people's children, and you work hard at it. Surely you would find it even more rewarding to teach your own son.'

When she gets insistent about something like this, there's no point in arguing, I thought. I decided I might as well give it a try. How difficult could it be to teach a second grader?

The first thing I did was to examine the second grade arithmetic textbook used in schools across the nation. I was surprised to find that in some ways I did not immediately understand it. Maybe it was because the book was different from the textbooks I had used when I was young, but simply opening it up and reading left me puzzled. I went back and read it from the beginning. Now it made sense. Yet when I looked at it from the point of view of a high school math teacher, there seemed to be an awful lot of things that were unnecessary for advancing to the higher grades of math. Who had prepared such a disorganized text?

You see, if elementary school arithmetic is to lead to high school mathematics, it must follow a certain logical order. I felt that the unnecessary parts should all be deleted and the order of presentation of the remaining material should be rearranged. I decided that the school text book was not the way to go. So I bought one of the commercially available math drill books and started Takeshi working with that.

But after only a short time I discovered that he was taking too much time to do things that were not particularly important. Naturally, that was no fun for him, and he was quickly losing interest in studying. I decided that even with these drill books he was wasting his study time and not developing the enjoyment of math that I had discovered early in life. Finally, having no other choice, I decided to create my own simple materials to help my son study.

I began by examining all the elementary and junior high school math texts from a high school teacher's perspective. What material is really necessary to give a student the ability to solve high school math easily? I eliminated material I considered to be a waste of time and expanded the points I thought were essential. Then I considered the order of presentation. I devised a natural progression that would take Takeshi step by step from the easiest arithmetic up to the more complex math functions that I was teaching in my regular high school classes.

As a teacher, I knew well enough that there isn't enough time to do adequate drill and practice in class, so I emphasized these features in the materials I began to create. I drew up dozens and dozens of calculation problems on both sides of loose leaf paper so that Takeshi would get plenty of drill on the most important elements in math. I made him do just one sheet of paper each day. Even with all those problems, the material was so similar that if he could do one problem he should be able to do all the problems on a single sheet.

As a result, he never spent more than 30 minutes a day on his new "homework." Because the material was clear and easy to follow and because the sheets I was making up could be finished so quickly, he did not develop an antagonism toward this study, but on the contrary grew to like it.

Each day he would do his work while my wife looked on, and then at night when I came home, I would mark the problems he had answered incorrectly. By seeing where he was having difficulty, I was able to make small adjustments on the next day's assignment.

The next day he would begin by correcting the problems I had marked wrong on his own. Then he would do the sheet assigned for that day. He continued to study like this, and I continued to create new homework for a few years. Still, he never spent more than half an hour on any one assignment and often much less. By the time he was in sixth grade he had completed the differential and integral calculus of the high school curriculum. I tried giving him a few college entrance examination problems and he was able to solve most of them with ease. I remember how relieved I felt that if he could handle this level of work while still an elementary school student, he would have no worries about math for the rest of his school life and need never fear the college entrance examinations.

Toru Kumon discovered at home the tremendous advantages of the "worksheets" he was creating. His son was learning at his own pace, for he could always go back and re-do sections he didn't understand completely, and the materials he was working on were designed to carry him steadily, step by step upwards toward higher level math. And yet, the work itself seemed painless, no more than 30 minutes a day. His son recognized his own progress in math, and as a result became motivated to advance even further. He learned the pleasure of self-study, of not being compared to anyone else in a classroom or a grade level.

The first worksheets were created in 1954. Only a year or

so later it was obvious that Takeshi was learning better than he ever had in school. Within another year, Toru Kumon's wife persuaded him to allow other children in the neighborhood to use the same worksheets he had developed for his own son. The results were much the same. In 1958 the Kumon Institute of Education was established in Osaka. In that first year, it attracted a total of 300 students just through the recommendations of parents whose children had improved by following Kumon's teaching method. The Kumon Institute was not a school, not a substitute for the public school system, but an adjunct to it, what we now call supplemental education. Kumon provided a specialized program in mathematics that seemed to work for students of all ages and all levels of ability.

In no time, the word spread beyond the city of Osaka. Only five years after setting up the company, the Kumon Institute had to open an office in Tokyo, and new Kumon "Centers" sprang up all over Japan. Although there are dozens of famous after-school education programs in Japan, Kumon soon became the nation's number one private educational program, with approximately 1.6 million students enrolled.

Although Kumon does not advertise the fact, it is no coincidence that at the very time the program was growing in Japan, international test comparisons showed that Japanese students consistently excelled in areas such as mathematics, in every case far outperforming children in North America and Europe. It was not long before the "secret" of the Kumon Method spread, and Kumon Centers began to spring up around the world. Just two decades after opening in Tokyo, the first Kumon Center opened in New York and a little while later in California. Thanks mostly to word-of-mouth recommendations from satisfied parents and interested teachers, the Kumon message spread across the U.S. and Canada and into Mexico. In addition, Kumon Centers opened in England, France, Germany, Switzerland, Austria, Belgium, Italy, Hong Kong, Taiwan, South Korea, Singapore, and Australia.

Just half a century after a modest high school math teacher designed some simple worksheets to help his son overcome his fear of math and become a good student, Kumon has become not only the largest supplemental education company in both

Japan and the United States, but the largest private educational institute in the world. And it is still growing.

Toru Kumon remained active in promoting and developing the program that he founded right up until his death in 1995. His son, Takeshi, gave up a promising career at one of Japan's top securities firms to return to the family business that he had helped to inspire. Tragically, he died of illness, and his younger brother, Hiroshi, took over as Chairman of the Kumon Institute of Education.

Today there are more than 24,000 Kumon Centers in 44 countries worldwide, helping over 3 million children every week "learn how to learn." Altogether, Toru Kumon's home-crafted approach to learning has already reached roughly 13 million students, and with the current rate of growth that number will double before very long.

Chapter 3

The Kumon Path
to Knowledge

There is nothing difficult, nothing strange or spooky about this
Kumon Method. It is, in its most fundamental aspect, just a
deep-set belief that children are incredibly special. All children.
And that, with just a little help from parents and friends, children
can develop in ways that will absolutely humble us.

It all started with a perfectly ordinary man with some perfectly ordinary children and some rather extraordinary ideas.
I had the wonderful opportunity to meet Toru Kumon many
years ago, and he was just as inspirational as I'd hoped he
would be. "The most important thing in the world," he said, is
to open up new worlds for our children to explore. He believed
that every child is a "gifted" child in ways we normally do not
appreciate. Every child possesses a vast, untapped potential to
learn. Every child has the potential to learn far beyond his or
her parents' expectations. "It is our job as educators," Kumon
said, "not to stuff knowledge into children as if they were
merely empty boxes, but to encourage each child to want to
learn, to enjoy learning and to be capable of studying whatever
he or she may need to or wish to in the future."

Toru Kumon understood that a child who has begun to learn mathematics or reading or music has become aware of his or her ability to learn and will almost surely expand that learning with each passing year. Moreover, those children who have learned through the Kumon Method have acquired more than knowledge. They have also learned concentration, and developed both good study skills and an ability to learn on their own.

In Kumon's experience, young children who are able to do high school level math are invariably children who like to read. Within only a few years they almost always demonstrate excellence in a number of other areas as well. Mr. Kumon said that children who can handle higher math at an early age will become outstanding all-around students later on. And he grounded his ideas not in theory, but in practice. He based his method on his own experience in teaching thousands of children and watching them grow, and in watching the results of hundreds of Kumon Centers teach hundreds of thousands of other children.

The Kumon Method:
Turning Students into Self-Learners

Most schools teach children on the basis of what all students of a certain age and grade are expected to learn. That is, a majority of children in any class should be able to finish each chapter and the entire textbook on the exact same schedule. Some may find it easy and some may find it difficult, but if everyone gets through a certain textbook by the end of the school year, they can all be expected to have a minimum level of knowledge. This attitude was certainly evident when I went to school, and probably was the same for you and your parents and grandparents.

Truly personalized, individual instruction is often rare because of class size and the considerable burden placed on most teachers to keep things moving. And, of course, the educational process is still directed by an adult, the teacher. Learning in school is teacher-driven, which can make the child a passive agent in the learning process.

Kumon turns the process upside-down. The goal of Kumon is to make learning a student-driven activity, to put the responsibility for learning on the learner, not on the teacher. Experience with millions of Kumon students has shown that learning occurs most efficiently when two criteria are met:

1) The level of the material to be learned corresponds exactly to the learner's level of ability, and
2) The student, not the teacher, controls the rate of progress.

Thus, the Kumon philosophy holds that if all students study at exactly the appropriate level they are much less likely to become discouraged, and so will more easily develop an enthusiasm for learning. The more they learn, the more they want to learn. Because the children set their own pace, there is no pressure to compete, and children discover that they want to do more because they enjoy what they are doing. As they develop other skills along the way, they begin to blossom, to grow towards their full potential.

Kumon aims to provide each child with a course of instruction that best meets his or her individual needs. This does not mean that the learning materials are custom-designed for each child. That would be wonderful, perhaps, but it is simply not possible. What Kumon gives to each child is a meticulously researched and refined path which can enable any student to climb from the most elementary basics up to the most advanced heights of a particular field of study. Kumon believes there is a natural sequence to learning a subject (especially math and reading) and that study should follow this order. Learning should proceed, as we noted before, like a narrow path up a steep mountain.

The Kumon path is composed of thousands of small steps that guide students forward little by little. The steps are the same for every student, but every child climbs at his or her own individual pace. There is no class to worry about, no pressure to keep up with anyone. Age and grade do not matter; just individual ability. This allows children to proceed at their own pace from beginning to end.

The child feels confident in moving from one step to the next because the steps are small. There is never a missed step. The incline varies constantly, sometimes steep and others times almost flat. Then, they are allowed to rest (by practicing work they are familiar with), and then challenged again.

In this way they are always able to absorb what they have learned and are always stimulated to go a little further.

Yet Kumon never pressures any student to advance. Only when the student has demonstrated complete mastery of the previous step is it time to move up to the next one. Thus, no student ever advances even the smallest step without having a rock-solid foundation for support. In climbing the Kumon path, the goal is not to get to the top of the mountain, nor to get there quickly. The goal is to advance at an incremental pace without any gaps in learning, to feel 100% confident about what you know and what you can do. How fast and how far one climbs is entirely up to each individual.

In Kumon, the written materials (called worksheets) take each child along this path independently, and the Instructor supplements the materials only when needed. While the body of materials is the same, each child is working at his or her own pace, and so is at a different point in the system. When the child wants input from the Instructor, it is always personal, geared to exactly what that child is studying.

When a student completes all 200 worksheets in a level, an achievement test follows. These tests consist of problems that use the skills developed in the previous level, as well as a few problems that draw upon skills learned earlier. In this way each student gets to review and reinforce the building blocks of math and reading skills and also to identify any points that might not be as strong as they were a few months ago. *The achievement tests confirm that a student has mastered the skills in a particular level and is ready to advance to the next level.*

Needless to say, this approach to learning is a big change from what the child is used to in school. Its primary function is to provide the most efficient, most individually satisfying learning system possible. However, this very approach to learning becomes a form of education in itself.

Children soon discover that learning requires effort and that no one else can make that effort for you. Either you work hard and produce results that you can be proud of or you don't.

Many parents say that, for whatever reason, this basic idea seems to have been lost over the years in the school system.

One Instructor put it this way, "In Kumon the child learns very early that he gets out of it only what he puts into it. That comes as a shock for some of today's children. There is no free lunch in Kumon. No one gets moved up to the next level simply because the class is moving up to the next grade. It's a very basic lesson in responsibility for one's own achievements, and I'm happy to say that children respond to it very well."

Schools and the
Educational Challenge of Tomorrow

If we as parents accept just a little part of Mr. Kumon's idealism, we must believe in the potential of children to grow. What, then, is more vital to each of us, and by extension to the future of our world, than a school? Each school represents our primary investment in the future of our community, our country, and ultimately, of the human race. Schools should be the most important buildings in any town—clean, well equipped, staffed by the best people available, and funded with every last dollar we can spare.

Yet teachers and parents alike recognize that schools are under tremendous pressure today. Many urban and rural schools are having their standardized test scores scrutinized and being called to task for the inordinate number of low achieving students. This can trigger a range of consequences, from being placed under the direct supervision of the superintendent to outright takeover by the state. Even more affluent suburban schools are being challenged to come up with ever-increasing amounts of funds to pay for good teachers and state-of-the-art facilities. Schools face an array of daunting problems from tight budgets to the intrusion of drugs and violence. Sadly, even the best educators find themselves limited by structural, economic and political realities, and that is just as true in Japan as it is in the U.S. or Canada or Mexico.

To take just a small example, if one looks in most school lobbies, you will see a display case filled with sports trophies. Last year's All-State football championship, All-County swim team, hockey team, basketball team, gymnastics team, maybe an award for the child setting new state records in track and field.

These are all worthy achievements and they deserve recog-

43

nition. But why are schools (and the communities they serve) so eager to place these achievements on a pedestal? "Of course, sports are an essential part of a child's growth," Mr. Kumon said, "and no school should ignore its duty to develop children's bodies as well as their minds. But it is ten times, a hundred times more important for schools to expand the scope of our children's mental abilities than to break records in athletic events."

I think what Mr. Kumon wanted me to understand was not that sports are bad, but rather that we spend too much time commemorating students' achievements from the past when we should be celebrating their potential to change the world in the future.

I remember my own school days very well, and I'm sure every other parent has similar memories. When I was in high school the personal computer did not exist, biotechnology was a dream, and lasers were used in laboratories, not in portable stereos at the beach. Being captain of the football team was probably as good a way to get a job back then as anything else.

Today, educators, economists and company executives all talk about the growth of a "knowledge-based society." What that means is that people with knowledge skills (financial services, computer programming, accounting, language skills, and so on) are much more in demand than people with trade skills (manufacturing, retail, and agriculture).

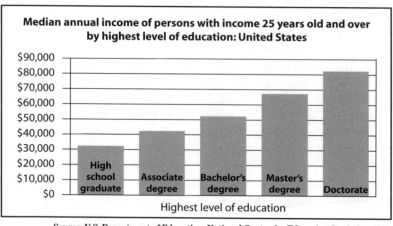

Source: U.S. Department of Education, National Center for Education Statistics, 1999.

It is safe to say that when our children grow up and have to look for work, all worthwhile jobs will be in what we now call "information intensive" or "high tech" fields. It is difficult for us to realize that many of the jobs our children will be applying for ten or twenty years from now do not even exist today. In that environment, initiative and the ability to acquire new knowledge will be just as important as their level of education.

In this sense, now as never before education is the single largest factor in determining our children's future. Yet, can we be sure that our children are receiving the knowledge and skills to prepare for the world they will soon face? My question is always, what will my child need to know? What information is essential for him to function reasonably well in the world he will grow up in—a world very different from what I see around me now?

The answer, of course, is that we don't know what information will be necessary 10 or 20 years from now. What we do know and can say with absolute certainty is that each child will need to *be able to learn* new information, to acquire new knowledge and to use new tools to survive and prosper in the future.

Will our children be adequately prepared? I don't know the answer to that. What I do know is that tens of thousands of parents from all walks of life are concerned enough to drive their children to Kumon Centers twice a week and to make sure they do 15 minutes of extra math and reading homework every day. It's a small price to pay for equipping children with essential academic skills and the ability to pursue knowledge and learning for the rest of their lives.

I know that the hard work I put into figuring things out on my own is for my benefit and my future. Working hard on my Kumon will help me in life.

– Alex Wan, Kumon student, Calgary, AB

Chapter 4

The Five Principles
of the Kumon Method

Many visitors, as well as some new Kumon parents, say they don't fully understand some of the program's basic concepts. After just a year or two in the program, however, most parents will tell you to stop worrying and trust Kumon. One parent I met had enrolled her eldest daughter in Kumon "to see how it goes," like putting a toe in the water; then, when she saw the results, she put her other three children into the program. This mom summed it up for all the thousands of parents who have had the same questions and concerns, only to have them disappear in the glow of their children's improving grades, test scores and self-confidence. "After all these years of constantly improving this system, you've got to believe the Kumon people have a pretty good idea what they're doing."

That's a great attitude, and it's my attitude now, but when I first came to Kumon I have to admit I was skeptical, too. Parents worry about doing what's right for our children. That's normal. As you learn more about Kumon and as you talk to other parents, you will find that you, too, will stop worrying and start watching your child advance through the program step by step.

There are several other fundamental principles in the Kumon Method that usually cause parents to ask "Why?" Your local Kumon Instructor will be happy to explain them, and any experienced Kumon parent you meet will tell you not to worry; everything in Kumon is there for a reason and it all works. I will give you my own take on these principles. Don't just read a book and think about it though: talk to a local Instructor and meet with other Kumon parents. They are in the best position to tell you why Kumon's principles are so important to success.

1) **Repetition: "Is This Really Necessary?"**

Why are we so worried about repetition in school? Every job I can think of requires at least some repetitive work, and we accept that as normal. We understand how vital repetition is in learning to play a sport or a musical instrument, but we still don't see how similar the situation is for academic subjects.

In math, the need for overlearning is the justification for repetition. Unlike other subjects, math skills must be overlearned at each stage in order for the student to be successful in later stages.

– Patricia L. Hollingsworth. Ph.D., Director,
The University School, Tulsa, OK

Repetition is one of the biggest problems parents seem to have with the Kumon Method (although it doesn't seem to bother the children much at all). As we have seen, Kumon requires repetition. Children have to do the same kind of problems again and again on a single worksheet, then do several more worksheets that are only slightly different. They then face very similar material in the worksheets that follow, then do even more of the same kind of work in the achievement test at the end of that level. This is not poor planning on the part of the Kumon design staff—just the reverse. Decades of study have shown that repetition is essential for students to learn the basics of any subject.

Consider math as an example. A child begins to learn addition with problems involving adding 1 to another number.

The first several worksheets will ask the student to add 1 (and always 1) to a long series of numbers. Of course, the child quickly masters that and goes on to the next step: adding 2 (and always 2) to a series of numbers. Accuracy is easy to achieve, and gradually the student understands this process of simple addition well enough that speed comes by itself. The child is then ready to move on.

Parents observing their children at play are probably already familiar with repetition in some form. How many times have we seen our children spend hours playing with something that we tired of watching in the first few minutes? Why do they ask us to read to them the same book over and over? The repetition of similar types of problems may appear to be less interesting and useful to the adult watching the work than the child who is doing it.

Moreover, the children delight in doing so many problems and getting all the answers right. They achieve visible mastery over something highly abstract, and both the Instructor and parents are full of praise.

For just this reason, the teacher who tries to "help" very young students by jumping quickly from one step to another is doing them a disservice. Trying to get the child to move quickly from adding 1 to adding 5 and then to adding 10 is like asking a young toddler to walk a few steps and then learn to run. A few may be able to do it, but the vast majority will stumble along, trying to please their teacher but afraid to say they don't really understand. This is precisely the situation that the Kumon Method is trying to avoid.

In fact, there is considerable research that supports the use of repetition to enhance skills and reinforce understanding. In an article that appeared in the Fall, 2002 issue of the journal *Education*, Professor David Weischadle cites research that "practice reinforces the learning and provides the students with an opportunity to relearn some steps he or she forgot. The learner becomes like the budding athlete who finds that he or she must practice and then, practice some more, to achieve competency." Any person who has ever attempted to learn a sport or musical instrument inherently understands the crucial role of practice and repetition to improve confidence and skills. The same holds true for the acquisition of language skills. The repetition of sentence patterns and substitution of nouns, adjectives or verb tense is a common strategy for studying a foreign language. Kumon's approach to the study of math and reading is similar.

Parents can best understand repetition by working with their child's Instructor to understand and adhere to the study goals that are established for each child. For example, when students enroll in Kumon they are given a placement test and begin from their 100% confidence level. The Instructor may feel comfortable assigning a full set of 10 sheets a day to the new student, knowing that the work will be easy. Thus, with 200 worksheets in each level, the Instructor can reasonably plan on the student taking 20 days to complete the initial level. Depending on the student, the Instructor may then plan on repeating the next level two times. If the student can continue to do a full set of 10 worksheets a day, we can estimate it will take 40 days to complete this second skill level (or, if the daily assignments are reduced to just five sheets, it will take 80 days). All of this, of course, depends on the individual child. The Instructor will create a study plan for each child based on their knowledge of the Kumon materials and the student's ability. Parents should stay aware of their children's progress, be patient and encourage their children as they steadily advance through the different skill levels.

Key point: Every child who has studied Kumon in the past 40+ years has had to go back and repeat many worksheets. This is an important part of the learning process. Repetition breeds improved understanding, which inevitably results in improved performance.

I didn't want a program that went just 2 days a week of class with nothing in between, or 1 hour a week of homework. I just didn't think that was enough. Not with math. I don't think schools give enough repetition with problems, not as much as when I was a child. I remember much more homework and getting up to the board and working problems as a child. One reason I started Kumon is that I looked in my child's classroom and I didn't see that.

– Kerri Niday, mother, Danville, CA

Repetition is good. At school they get one page with 15 math problems. Not enough to reinforce anything. It may seem tedious to watch, but the children really learn their facts.

— **Suzanne Schembri-Coffin, mother, Danville, CA**

I don't blame the teachers. They have to move on, they have so many subjects to cover. But here [at Kumon] they are so specific and they know exactly where your child's weak points are and they repeat until he or she masters it. Then he or she can move on at his or her own pace and master it at the same time.

My son always made mistakes in class; I always thought they were lots of silly mistakes. He could see the right answer later, but he didn't know why he made these silly mistakes. We brought him to Kumon and that's the first thing he got straight – no more silly mistakes. I found that with the repetition he does in Kumon, he gets it. When he comes here, he repeats until he masters it and then he gets to go to the next level.

— **Lesley Mafi, mother, Sacramento, CA**

2) **Speed: "Why Must Kumon Be Timed?"**

While insisting on accuracy is not unusual, Kumon's emphasis on a certain degree of speed in completing everything is one of the features that sets it apart from many other educational programs. For that reason, and because this element of the Kumon Method can be misunderstood, let's look at it in more detail.

In Kumon, the target time range is referred to as the *standard completion time*, or SCT. The SCT is the amount of time in which a student must complete a given worksheet with a 100% score. As you would expect with Kumon, the SCT is the product of considerable study. Rather than setting an SCT range for each level of 200 worksheets, Kumon has calculated a target time range for every set of 10 worksheets. When a student can answer all the problems in a set correctly, and is able to do so within a reasonable period of time, it is clear that he or she is ready to take a small step up to the next set.

The SCT is not used for the pre-school levels. There is no time limit for the three introductory levels in either math or reading. The SCT for the early levels runs from half a minute to 2 minutes per worksheet. Beginning with Level B, as the problems become more challenging, the SCT naturally becomes longer, rising to 3-5 minutes, then 5-7 minutes, and in the very highest levels of math and reading, up to 30-60 minutes for a single worksheet.

The Standard Completion Time is based on studies of lots of students doing the same work. Not a few hundred or a few thousand students, but literally millions of children worldwide. These times reflect average completion times for students who have successfully mastered the material involved at each level, and they have been refined again and again to make them more realistic. The SCT is not designed to be too easy or too difficult. These times are practical guidelines that make students concentrate on completing their work while still remaining accurate.

Some parents are concerned with Kumon's emphasis on time, and understandably so. Especially in teaching elementary school students, for example, it is natural to question how Kumon can reconcile its belief that education must be interesting and help to motivate the child with its insistence that students meet fixed time guidelines.

Kumon is not trying to pressure students or to make them race through their daily assignments. The idea of speed itself as a goal has no meaning. The purpose of the SCT is to show clearly that a student has mastered one step of the learning process and is ready to go on to the next. Remember we said that a student who completes 70% or 80% or even 90% of a worksheet or a test accurately is still not ready to move on? Likewise, the child who can get 100%, but only after an unusually long time thinking about it has not shown a real mastery of the material.

Let's look at a simple example. Suppose your daughter is working with addition. Her worksheets require her to add 8 + 2, 9 + 2, and so on. She can figure out the answers eventually by counting on her fingers. That's fine. It means she understands the concept of addition. But just arriving at the right answer doesn't mean she has "learned" addition in a way that will be useful to her in the future.

When she encounters more complicated math in school or in a real world situation, she will not have time to count on her fingers; she won't even have time to use a calculator.

To master addition means to be able to produce sums in your head instantaneously. When you say to her "8 + 2" and she does not immediately answer "10!" you know that she has not mastered that addition fact. Let's imagine that she took 10 seconds to give you the answer. You would know instinctively that something was wrong. We assume it takes time for a young child to be able to verbalize an answer. But if she takes more than a reasonable amount of time, say, more than five or ten seconds in this case, it means she still needs more practice in basic addition.

The same principle is applied to the Kumon Reading program, where every level has an SCT, and specific sections of the worksheets require separate timed reading aloud. Dr. Jay Samuels, a Professor of Educational Psychology at the University of Minnesota, said that "if a person could recognize words in print with little or no effort the bulk of their cognitive skills could be focused on meaning." His research suggests that "repeated reading will build accuracy and fluency in reading."

In essence, the standard completion times are very much like this example. That is, the SCT for any group of worksheets is not a specific target time, not some arbitrary goal that your child must meet. Instead, it is a target time *range* which has been shown to be a realistic goal for millions of students. In other words, Kumon does not say: "This worksheet must be completed in one and a half minutes." Rather, the SCT range indicates that any student around the world who really understands the material at that level should be able to finish the worksheet in somewhere between 2 to 4 minutes. Many will finish closer to 2 minutes and some closer to 4. A student who takes 5 or 6 minutes to do the same work is not yet really comfortable with the material. Decades of study with millions of children have shown that these completion ranges are reasonable and that almost all children will attain them with ease.

In addition to assessing a level of understanding, the SCT has another purpose—one that becomes increasingly important the further a student goes in school. The emphasis on working within a fixed time frame helps children learn to work efficiently. As they progress through Kumon, children are unconsciously learning the importance of focusing their attention on the task at hand, of using their work time productively. As we noted in the Introduction, testing is a fact of life for every child, and the older they get, the more tests they are going to encounter. Learning to think clearly and to efficiently use a fixed time limit is a key element to being able to perform well on tests of all sorts in years to come.

Simply put, the ability to work quickly and accurately is one of the most important study skills any child can learn. Combine that speed and accuracy with a thorough understanding of the material being tested, and the results are outstanding.

My Allison was always a bit of a day-dreamer. Kumon helped her to focus. The SCT is very helpful. She learned to sit down, focus and do her work within set time limits. The ability to focus is a huge benefit of Kumon. It has done great things for all my children for different reasons. People see my Allison and put their own children in Kumon.

– Dina Friedman, mother, Toronto, ON

---

3) Accuracy: "Isn't a '95' Good Enough?"

There are two ways that an Instructor can be sure that a student has mastered one stage of work and is ready to move up to the next: accuracy and speed. Neither one alone is sufficient to give a student the green light. Speed without accuracy is just sloppy work, and accuracy without a reasonable amount of speed is proof of a *lack* of mastery. Kumon uses both to measure mastery and to ensure that a student has the skills required to move ahead.

Most people probably feel that accuracy on tests and homework should be one of the primary criteria to judge whether or not a student understands material. For many parents, a score of 90 or above is a sign that a student "gets it" and is ready to advance. I think most parents would say, "There is so much material that children need to study. Once a student can score 95, and do so consistently, it's time to move on to harder lessons."

Kumon completely agrees with the underlying principle. Where Kumon differs is in the definition of "mastery." There is a lot of material to study in both mathematics and reading and the natural approach is, "first you master step one, then you go on to step two." In Kumon, getting 95% right is wonderful; but it doesn't show mastery. Sure, only a few mistakes, but one or two mistakes show a gap in understanding. Maybe that gap is very small, but down the road a complex word problem could hinge on the student's ability to perform exactly that small function that he or she is getting wrong today. Kumon believes that a student's ability to identify mistakes *and* correct them are critical steps in demonstrating mastery.

Kumon does not allow for making excuses or telling children "that's good enough." Kumon promises one thing to any child who follows the program diligently (and to his or her parents): complete understanding of basic skills. No compromises. No gaps. No "almosts." In Kumon, students are permitted to move on only after demonstrating mastery by achieving 100% within the SCT. Perfect scores, of course, are not always achieved on the first attempt. 100% is a goal that students work toward. Mistakes, after all, are only wrong until corrected.

This is a big part of the Kumon philosophy. Tackling challenging work, struggling with it to some degree, and then mastering it are experiences that build character, confidence *and* better math and reading skills. When the student hits 100%, he or she knows it and is proud of the result. When they know that every level that they advance in the program is the result of 100% accuracy on the levels below, they develop a confidence that very, very few programs can offer.

Again, go back to Toru Kumon's belief: children are capable of much more than we believe. We should not settle for "good enough" work when they are capable of perfection.

A Footnote on Speed and Accuracy
Clearly, the Kumon Method emphasizes accuracy (100% understanding) and speed (Standard Completion Time ranges) in just the same way that you did when you asked your daughter to add 8 + 2 in her head. If she doesn't get the right answer or takes too long to arrive at the right answer, you know that something is wrong, either with her basic knowledge or with the process

she uses to calculate the answer. The combination of speed and accuracy is a simple, effective way to measure understanding.

But there is something more, something quite important that both parents and children talk about all the time: the benefits of becoming totally accustomed to displaying your knowledge quickly and accurately when the clock is ticking. Toru Kumon was certainly not trying to teach children how to perform well on timed tests, but at least a few million parents are very, very glad that his system has produced such a useful fringe benefit.

Parents know that every test children take these days is timed, from placement tests for kindergartens to the SATs for college entrance. Yet so many children tend to "freeze up" in timed tests or make silly mistakes under pressure that the tests do not reflect their real level of ability. Kumon children don't have that problem. Everything is timed right from Day 1, so they are used to the idea of working efficiently to perform their best on a timed test.

Whenever I interview children in Kumon Centers, I always ask about tests they take in school, not just their regular subject exams but also the many kinds of standardized achievement tests that schools put children through these days. They all say—and by "all" I mean without a single exception—that regardless of the material, the process of test-taking itself is easy.

One 13-year-old who had just finished a whole day of standardized testing in school put it nicely for more than 100,000 of his peers in North America. When I asked him what it was like taking a battery of timed tests, he just waved his hand as if brushing the whole idea aside and answered, "Cake." (For those of you who don't speak Teenager, I think that means it was a piece of cake.) Children all over the U.S. and Canada tell me exactly the same thing.

You have to have speed to do calculations, whether it's science or whatever. I don't want them to be bogged down doing the simple calculations when they have to be looking at the big picture. I want that to come easy.

– Wendy Ichiuji, mother, Danville, CA

---

4) **Independent Learning Skills**

We noted in Chapter 2 that the Kumon Method is an individual path to knowledge. It is not custom-designed for each child, but designed so that each child can work at his or her own pace, with no reference to other students, age groups, classes, etc. In this sense, Kumon offers the ideal system for individual achievement.

Consider this story from Toru Kumon. It goes back to the 1950s, when he was still a high school math teacher, creating problem sheets (what would later become worksheets) to help his eldest son learn the basics of high school math in elementary school. This episode comes from a time when the boy was in 5th grade; having studied at home with his father for about three years:

> I thought it would be better in many respects if my son had a chance to listen to high school lessons rather than mainly using self-study materials. I often wondered if the study method I had adopted would be inefficient, particularly when new topics were introduced. It turned out, however, that my son actually spent far less time studying compared to the average 9th and 10th grader and that his academic ability was just as good. This fact was a surprise for me since I had believed that lecture-style teaching was more effective than self-study. *Only then did I realize that giving him time to solve problems by himself was better than having him attend lectures.* After this, I handed my freshman high school students some rewritten study materials and let them study with less explanation. My students came to enjoy this, and my new teaching style proved to be more effective (emphasis added).

From this point on, Toru Kumon realized the importance of self-study, or independent learning, as it is sometimes called. He understood that even young children have potential to study on their own, to solve problems that they have never been told explicitly how to solve. From this revelation sprang the beginnings of the Kumon Method, the idea of a carefully constructed learning system with meticulous attention to the printed materials, but no need for traditional teachers to tell students how to do their work. The learning process is left in the hands of the student, with a trained Instructor available, but as a guide, not a lecturer. By watching his own child, Toru Kumon discovered that learning can be interesting, even fun, for children as long as it is an adventure.

This discovery was so important that it changed Mr. Kumon's thinking forever. Self-learning became the cornerstone of the method he was developing. He later wrote, "The essence of the Kumon Method is allowing students to advance through self-study. *Getting children to recognize that they can advance without being taught is the most important thing at Kumon.*"

Mr. Kumon realized that the most important challenge for Instructors is to show children that they can climb the path of knowledge on their own. This is what independent learning is all about. If you teach him or her *how to learn*, it is like teaching someone how to fish: they will never go hungry. A child who *learns how to learn* is transformed—from a passive vessel into a self-motivated, self-actuated *learner*. Such a child can approach problems he or she has never faced before and figure out ways to solve them.

There is an infinite amount of information in the world. We will never be able to teach children all of it. What we need to do is teach them how to learn by themselves, and this actually involves developing strong character traits that enable them to become life-long learners... Self-learning ability is a necessity in high school. If students don't have self-learning skills and confidence beforehand, they will be in trouble. Many high school textbooks contain a lot of information that the teacher won't have time to go through completely. Students are often expected to figure out a lot on their own, and high school texts can be confusing. Toru Kumon always said, "Kumon is the kindest method of learning." I think of that when I look at high school texts. They are not a kind or easy place to hone your self-learning skills. But if students already have those skills from Kumon, they can apply them in high school. That's how Kumon makes high school easier—it makes students fearless when encountering challenges.

– Phyllis Peyron, Kumon Instructor, San Francisco, CA

Tutoring may be fine for some things, but no tutor can go to school with a child, no tutor can go into the exam room with the child. *Kumon enables students to be independent. That is very important.*

— *Faye Komagata, Kumon Instructor, Honolulu, HI*

When you add to this independent learning a solid foundation of study habits and a maturing sense of self-confidence (both essential building blocks of Kumon), a child who has become a self-learner is ready to handle whatever kind of educational challenge comes along. The competition is not about grades (believe me; I used to work in an Ivy League Admissions Office). Most colleges assume children have good grades. What universities want are students who know how to think, act and solve problems on their own initiative, without having to be told what to do by a teacher (come to think of it, isn't that what most employers are looking for?).

Debbie Tajiri, a Kumon Instructor in Hawaii, said it this way, "The ability to self-learn enables a child to have more options in life and opens the door of opportunity that much wider." And that, too, is what Kumon is all about.

5) **Advancing Beyond Grade Level**

Let's follow Mr. Kumon's thought a little further on this topic of self-study. He points out, just as we noted before, that students who are self-learners are prime candidates to get into good universities, and then he goes a step beyond in his thinking:

> Our aim should be to educate our students so well through the Kumon Method that they don't have to depend solely on classroom activities to be able to deeply understand the course content. Students who develop this capacity will have a good chance to enter leading universities. To make this possible, we must help students acquire the ability of self-study from an early age *and accelerate their level of study beyond their school grade*. (Emphasis added)

This last line is the key. It follows that if Kumon teaches children to become independent learners, some of them will learn at a faster pace than their peers. This is certainly what happened to Mr. Kumon's own son, who was doing high school-level work while still in the 5th grade. Multiply that times millions of students and you have a lot of children who are studying way beyond their "normal" school level.

Mr. Kumon recognized that self-learners are motivated by their own progress. It is only natural when climbing a mountain to look up and see what lies ahead. Students don't need to be pushed to scale these heights, but they do need to recognize that there are concrete goals and interesting challenges ahead. For that reason, it is important to encourage study of materials above the current grade level.

The biggest problem, in Mr. Kumon's view, was not getting children to want to tackle the challenges of advanced study, but getting parents and Instructors to believe that it was possible and desirable:

> The most important and difficult feature for people to understand about the Kumon Method is having students advance beyond their actual school grade. The majority of people don't have the experience of studying material beyond their school grade. Consequently, they don't believe that children have that ability. Even Instructors find this fact hard to believe at first. The history of the Kumon Method can be called the history of our efforts to convince people of this fact.

That was written many years ago, but the same problem still exists. Many parents just don't believe that children can study beyond what is considered a "normal" level for them, or that it isn't "natural" for them to do so. If they see examples of children who are progressing at a faster-than-normal rate, they are inclined to say "The parents are pushing them too hard" or "That just isn't normal." In fact, advancing beyond grade level is a normal consequence of consistent, long-term Kumon study. Every year more and more young children in Kumon show that what we expect as "normal" for a certain age is more a reflection of the limits we have put on children than anything inherent in the child's ability to learn. More Kumon parents are spreading the word that what is really "normal" is for a child to be learning a wide variety of things, not under pressure or stress, but because children naturally enjoy learning about the world around them.

This is especially true of younger children. Dr. Ryuta Kawashima, a Professor of Medicine at Japan's Tohuku University, has studied the development of the brain. He has found that "if children learn a little of the basics every day, doing calculations or reading out loud, they will activate their developing brains which will in turn grow soundly."

In Missouri, I met a wonderful couple, Dr. and Mrs. Figenshau. At the time, their son and daughter were both six years old and attending a local kindergarten. They had also been doing Kumon for over a year. Susan Figenshau said very matter-of-factly, "When we went to kindergarten orientation, the teachers explained that the goal of the math curriculum is to have the children count to 100 by the end of the year. I shared this information with my children. They could not believe it. Karen told her teacher how proud she is that she can already do 2nd grade math."

In New Jersey I met a 7-year-old named Jeffrey Chien who had been studying Kumon for about two years. Kumon has really developed his love for reading. Now his Mom says he reads 200 books in a summer. Is that unusual? Certainly. Is it strange? Not at all. Jeffrey has discovered the joy of reading, and Kumon has given him a path to expand that talent as far as he wants. Mrs. Chien told me, "His teacher says that according to some scale the average reading level in his class is 5 or 6, but Jeffrey's level is about 36." Performing at a level far beyond his peers is "normal" for this boy, and if he continues to study without pressure or interference, there is no limit to how far he can go.

Are most of the Kumon children who are studying one, two or three grade levels beyond their normal school level geniuses? I posed that question to Stan Laser, a former math and science teacher and later vice principal of Brooklyn High School in New York, where he was in charge of 1,200 students. Stan, who is now a Kumon Instructor, said that very few of the children who outperform later on are abnormally bright at an early age. "I sometimes ask the parents of children who turn out to be superstars in Kumon if those children were exceptionally bright when they were very young. Did they play with numbers or show other abilities at an early age to indicate their potential? In almost every case the parents say no, my child was just an average child." In other words, the great majority of the children who excel in elementary school or junior high are not geniuses. Their growth and success in attaining higher levels of ability has emerged through regular study.

All of this would have Toru Kumon nodding and smiling with a knowing look on his face. Isn't it obvious, he would say to us? Children are not only capable of advanced study, but need to be given the opportunity to advance. But, as Mr. Kumon reminisces below, it took time for him to understand this process:

> Initially, it was difficult to determine how children who advanced to higher levels would develop. Many Instructors worried that letting children advance so far would bring about other problems. But as children advance so far, they naturally develop self-motivation and acquire self-esteem and self-confidence because of their abilities.
>
> Everyone thinks it is perfectly natural when children who were exceptional when they started Kumon eventually move beyond their actual school grade. But if Instructors see that children who had average abilities at the beginning also advance by the same process, they will have a more profound understanding of the learning effect of the Kumon Method.

Attaining "G by 5"

Kumon does not push children to advance, but Kumon does encourage children to set goals for themselves. Kumon Instructors reward performance and they often find that the child's own sense of satisfaction is a prime motivator. In other words, children who do well want to keep doing well; children who begin to advance in their studies want to advance further.

One potential goal for Kumon students is to reach Level G, which is a fairly advanced level, by the fifth grade in school, or approximately age 10. This "G by 5" or "G5" is something you may hear mentioned when you visit a Kumon Center. Instructors often talk about children attaining G5 or being "on track" to hit G by 5. However, you should not think that this is the whole focus of Kumon. G5 is just a marker or a milestone of achievement, not a FINISH line by any means. It shows that certain students (most likely children who begin at an early age and continue in the program for a few years) are advancing in a strong, steady fashion. That means they have already acquired good study habits, they have learned all the basics up to Level G, and they are ready to move on to higher and higher levels of study.

There is another, quite serious aspect to G by 5, however. Level G is a key point in both the math and reading programs. In math, it marks the introduction of algebra, and in reading this is where students learn key summarizations skills. In many ways, Level G marks the beginning of higher-level study. Many students who have never experienced difficulty in elementary school math and reading may find junior high school work very challenging: the pace picks up, grading becomes stricter in schools, and students' social activities begin to compete with academics. By reaching Level G by the fifth grade—roughly two years ahead of grade level—Kumon gives students an edge when they need it most. It helps children to avoid the frustration that is so common in making the transition from elementary to junior high school, and guarantees that there are no dangerous gaps in learning as children begin to tackle advanced materials like algebraic equations and critical reading.

Many parents do not realize just how important this can be. In a special "white paper" a few years ago, the U.S. Department of Education noted that

> Algebra is the 'gateway' to advanced mathematics and science in high school, yet most students do not take it in middle school. Students who study algebra in middle school and who plan to take advanced mathematics and science courses in high school have an advantage. Students who take rigorous mathematics and science courses are much more likely to go to college than those

who do not. [In particular,] low-income students who took algebra I and geometry were almost three times as likely to attend college as those who did not.

The then-Secretary of Education, Richard Riley, wrote in the report:

The key to understanding mathematics is taking algebra or courses covering algebraic concepts by the end of the 8th grade. Achievement by that stage gives students an important advantage in taking rigorous high school mathematics and science courses.

(*Mathematics Equals Opportunity*, U.S. Department of Education, 1997.)

If your child, for whatever reason, does not attain G by 5, that absolutely does *not* have any negative implications. G5 is a convenient way to highlight children who are on track to complete junior high-level work early, and Kumon naturally hopes that more and more children will be attaining G5 every year. But the whole message of the Kumon philosophy is that children develop at different rates and they need to be given the freedom to do that. Your child might just miss reaching Level G by fifth grade but attain it the next year, which will still be of tremendous help in junior high. He or she might not hit G5 but eventually go on to much higher levels of study than some other children who did make G5. It is always important to set targets for your children and allow them to work at their own pace to attain those goals.

My son, Santiago, was in a Montessori program before. He was a year behind the other children when he started kindergarten. His teacher told me he needed some special help. I heard about Kumon from a friend and I put him in this Center. Now he reads children's books by himself. Recently he took some kind of placement test with a maximum score of 79.7; he got a 79.5. His teacher was amazed. I told her he is doing Kumon, and she said, "Of course. Kumon is the best."

– Martha Casamayor, mother, Miami, FL

Parents attend an orientation session prior to enrolling a child in Kumon. Here an Instructor and parents discuss the goals that have been set for their child and the parents' important role in achieving them.

When students visit the Kumon Center, they hand in homework and find their folder with that day's class work and new homework assignments.

A Kumon Center is like a library or a study hall where children of different ages work and progress at an individualized pace. Here we see some students completing their work while others are making corrections under the watchful eyes of Kumon Assistants.

CDs are used to reinforce the contents of the reading materials. Students read along with the CD and repeat sounds, words and sentences.

Students spend about 15–20 minutes a day per subject on the Kumon assignments. This boy is engaged in his math, while his reading assignment awaits his attention.

Kumon students are required to practice reading aloud using brief passages from the worksheets or a book from the Recommended Reading List. Oral reading is essential for checking comprehension and developing fluency with written passages.

Reworking incorrect problems is an essential part of Kumon study. Students can only advance after correcting all mistakes and achieving 100% accuracy.

Kumon Instructors keep detailed records of every student's performance on the daily assignments. Kumon has recently developed software that allows Instructors to readily access student records and to chart current performance and future progress.

Kumon students can be an example and an inspiration to younger siblings. It is common for little brothers and sisters to want their own homework and to ask parents if they can do Kumon too.

More and more parents are seeing the benefits of enrolling their children in Kumon before they begin kindergarten.

One of the big goals of the Kumon Method is to train children to focus, concentrate and study.

Kumon Centers use manipulatives like Kumon's Magnetic Number Board to help students learn sequencing, number facts and develop tactile skills.

Kumon's Alphabet Board supplements the reading worksheets by allowing students to work with letters and practice sounding them out.

Kumon's Annual Math Challenge is held on college campuses throughout Canada and the United States. Thousands of Kumon students and their peers from surrounding communities compete for college scholarships and other prizes.

Families enjoy the recognition their children receive at Kumon Awards Ceremonies. Students are awarded ribbons or medals for achievements in math, reading and other significant accomplishments.

Kumon Instructors attend workshops, seminars and conferences to learn about developments in education, improvements to the Kumon curriculum, and to share research conducted at Centers in their area.

Chapter 5

How Does Kumon Work?

Let's assume that you've heard about Kumon from a friend or neighbor, or perhaps you've read about it in the newspaper. It sounds interesting, but you're not ready to make a decision about something as important as your child's education just on hearsay. You'll probably want to talk to someone who really knows about Kumon and perhaps you'll want to see it in action. You are not alone. At every Kumon Center I visited, I found parents looking for first-hand information about the program.

The Kumon organization encourages this. They are confident that the more you know about Kumon, the more convinced you will be that this is the right thing for your child. So by all means, visit your local Kumon Center, and while you are there, ask lots of questions. No one will make you feel awkward for asking questions. I have never met a Kumon Instructor who wasn't happy to talk about the program with interested parents.

Instructors realize that enrolling in Kumon is an important decision and a serious commitment for parents. To assist them, Instructors require a half-hour or so pre-enrollment orientation meeting. This is an opportunity for parents to learn how Kumon works and for the Instructor to hear about each family's needs and expectations. The Instructor will go over the Kumon Method with you, explain how that particular Center operates, and make sure that you understand the very important role you, the parent, play in helping your child "learn how to learn" with Kumon.

Your local Instructor can explain things much better than I can. For those of you who may not have a chance to visit a Kumon Center right away, I will explain some of the basics of how Kumon works in practice.

First Step: Finding the "Just Right" Place to Start

One of the greatest strengths of the Kumon Method is the emphasis it places on individualized learning. That does not mean that the Instructor sits with a single child all the time in a one-on-one setting. Individualized learning means that each child starts at the "just right" step on the long staircase of worksheets, and climbs at his or her own pace. In other words, Kumon carefully matches the level of the instructional materials to each individual's unique abilities.

Obviously, one of the most important steps in that matching of materials and ability is choosing where to start climbing. There are thousands of worksheets in both the math and reading programs. Where should a child start? Should the Instructor simply interview the child (or the parents) and choose what seems to be a good starting point? Kumon says no. Instructors are talented, but it is impossible to know accurately what a child does and doesn't know on the first day at a Kumon Center.

Some parents say the starting point is obvious. They say their children should start right where they are in their school classes—especially if they're getting good grades already—and go on from there. Many Instructors hear parents new to the Kumon program say things like "My son knows multiplication inside-out" or "My daughter is doing fractions in school; at least you should start her with fractions. . . ." That sounds reasonable, doesn't it?

Mechanically starting with whatever material the child is studying in school would be just as big a mistake as having the

Instructor try to guess where the child should begin. Remember, the goal of the Kumon Method is for students to master a skill and to demonstrate mastery by completing similar types of problems within an allotted time frame. A "reasonably good understanding" of something won't cut it; Kumon aims for mastery and nothing less. To use reading as an example, a student may know some very impressive vocabulary words without knowing the basics of sentence-building that are essential to use those words.

Kumon uses its own placement tests to determine the best starting point for each child. It is not an IQ test, not a standardized test in the school sense, not a way to judge whether your child is "gifted" or "challenged," or any attempt to label your child. The sole purpose of Kumon's placement test is to find exactly where to start an incoming student in order to achieve maximum results. The tests are short and painless. There are no "trick" questions. The tests are designed to show the achievement level at that point in time.

The tests—like all exercises in Kumon—are timed. For example, a student who can answer 60 addition problems correctly, but who needs 20 minutes to do it, or has to count on his fingers, has not mastered addition despite a 100% score. Thus, even among several children scoring equally on the same test, it is possible to differentiate their levels of ability.

The Kumon Method assumes that every *child has enormous potential to learn and to grow.* The placement test only shows from what step on the staircase a child will begin climbing. Since each child is an individual in Kumon, not a member of a class, each has his or her own staircase to climb, at his or her own pace.

What is a Comfortable Starting Point?

Let's say you take your child to a Kumon Center. The first thing that happens is that the Instructor will administer a short placement test. Your child will probably find it simple and straightforward, and since there is no pressure, it is a low-stress event.

If stress comes, I'm sad to say, it is usually from the parents. Parents may be surprised, possibly shocked when the Instructor tells you at what level your child should begin to study Kumon. I think I have had about a thousand parents tell me something like: "My daughter is doing long division in school, but Kumon made her start with addition!"

I had the same reaction when my own son started Kumon. I had heard stories of children studying way beyond their school grade level. I didn't expect my son to be doing calculus in the 3rd grade, but I did hope he would get a little edge on his school work and have an easier time in school. So we went to the local Kumon Center and took the placement test, and guess what? The Instructor wanted my son to start with the same material he was doing *last year* in school. I didn't realize that there were basic skills he hadn't mastered yet.

Fortunately, the Instructor was right there for me. She knew what I was thinking before I said a word. "Relax," she told me, "There's nothing wrong. Your son is just as bright as you thought he was, probably much brighter. I can't guarantee how fast or how far he will go in this course, but I can guarantee you that nothing in Kumon will slow him down. He will succeed to the limit of his potential, and you will be amazed at what he achieves in the next year or so, believe me."

She patiently explained that the comfortable starting point was intended to give him a 'running start' and the momentum needed to advance smoothly through more challenging materials ahead. It also allows him to ease into the routine of doing the assignments on a daily basis. "And," she said, with a poignant look in my direction, "we want to get his parents used to checking his homework every night and your son to get used to having his dad praise him for turning in perfect homework regularly."

Then she explained that nothing is done in Kumon just because it seems to be right. The Kumon philosophy is wonderful in theory, but the theory would mean little without years and years of practice—of implementation, analysis and research. Kumon has studied the results of millions of children and found out what works best. In short, Kumon Instructors follow the method for a very good reason: *it works*.

In fact, veteran Instructors are forever advising new ones, "If you have any doubts or questions about how to do something, go back to the Kumon Method, because everything is there for a reason. Trust the Kumon Method. The Kumon Method says, 'Start a child at just the right level and everything proceeds smoothly. Start a child too high or too low and you guarantee frustration and resistance to learning.'

Yet despite having said all this, and despite the assurances of Kumon Instructors around the world, thousands of parents are absolutely shocked to discover how "low" on the scale their children are supposed to start. "Did my child fail the placement test?" they ask. The answer is no, your child did very well. Your child has shown exactly what he or she does and doesn't understand about the test subject(s), and by doing so has indicated where he or she will feel completely comfortable and confident beginning the program. If we expect the child to come to the Center every week, do daily homework, and make a serious effort to learn, he or she must feel comfortable from the beginning of the program right to the end.

Kumon calls this idea the *Comfortable Starting Point*. What it all boils down to is that it is essential to start each child at a skill level that is comfortable right from the start. If your child finds the starting level a little too easy, that's fine; the super-easy work will pass quickly.

My son's Kumon Instructor put it like this:

> He will go through that level quickly and then progress to the next level. In time you will find him doing work that is more advanced than what he is doing in school. But it must come 'naturally,' that is, in a long series of tiny steps forward from a foundation where he feels totally confident. During the first couple of months, while he is learning to do homework every day and getting accustomed to the Kumon program, the work will seem easy and will flow smoothly, which will mean less stress for him and for you.

Dean Bradley, Vice President of Instruction and Research for North America, puts it this way:

> We start children at a point where we *know* they're going to be achievers. Look at math, for example. We can take a child who hates math, who hates anything to do with math, and start him or her at such a basic

point that a single day's work takes about six minutes. You get a child doing that regularly and right away you'll see a sense of accomplishment developing. The child thinks, 'I hate math, but I can do this stuff easily and I'm getting 100% right. What's the big deal?' That confidence carries him or her into the next unit and then into the next level, and before they know it, children discover that they're actually good at math.

In a study prepared for the Hawaii Department of Education, researchers found that 79% or more of the Kumon students responded positively to the following statements:

a. I find math more interesting since I started Kumon.

b. I am better at solving problems since I started Kumon.

c. Kumon has helped me improve my study habits.

d. I am learning to work hard since I started Kumon.

e. I do better in my regular math class since I started Kumon.

f. My speed of doing math has increased since I started Kumon.

(*Evaluation of the After School Instruction Program Kumon Mathematics Pilot Program*, Nancy C. Whitman, et al, Department of Curriculum and Instruction, College of Education, University of Hawaii, November 1993.)

Kumon has long advocated education which serves children above anybody else. Children start at a level which is just right for them. This "just right" learning which Kumon has advocated is the result of serious thought about what is important to children, about what will be useful to children in the future, and about how to contribute to the lives of children.

– Toru Kumon

Materials

Kumon has no textbooks, no workbooks, and no required reference books. The instructional materials are 5½ × 8 inches double-sided worksheets, so the only tools you need to do Kumon are a pencil and an eraser. The worksheets, though small and simple in appearance, have proven powerful instruments for changing the lives of children throughout the world. Kumon has spent decades, not just a few years, developing and refining their unique copyrighted learning materials.

There are thousands of worksheets for both the math program and the reading program, organized into "sets" of 10 worksheets, with 20 sets to a "level." There are 23 levels of 200 worksheets for the math program, and 22 levels for reading. Each level is identified by a letter. Letters which are multiples of A indicate early levels and they proceed in a natural sequence up into the alphabet. Thus, for example, after Level 5A comes 4A, then 3A, 2A, and then A, B, C, etc. By using this system, the student, the Instructor and the parent know exactly where the child is within the Kumon system. An Instructor might say, for example, "She did very well on B71-80, so I want her to try B81-90 today," and you, the parent, will know exactly what that means because you are watching your child complete the assignments every day. This system makes it easy to spot micro-changes in a child's progress, and also to spot weaknesses if they occur. Many parents say that knowing with such precision where their child is in the system is a great relief, quite unlike the "I wonder what she's doing in school these days?" feeling that so many of us have about our children in regular school.

At this writing, the reading program goes through Level K and math through Level Q. Both programs may be extended in the coming years as more and more students progress up the Kumon ladder and are ready to take on more challenging work.

Now let's look at the content of the worksheets.

Obviously, the content of the math and reading worksheets is very different, but the fundamental approach is the same. When a new skill is introduced in Kumon, there are no lengthy pages of explanation. Instead, an example of the new principle is printed at the top of a worksheet, sometimes with a brief explanation, together with a sample problem/sentence or two. The first several problems/questions that follow are very close to the example so that students quickly build confidence in working with the new principle. In the subsequent worksheets, problems are less and less like the example, challenging students to incorporate what they have learned. This is the process that underlies the Kumon approach to introducing new concepts.

Particularly with the math program, some parents question why Kumon does not "teach" concepts as they are taught in school. It is important to understand that Kumon does not avoid concepts; quite the contrary, it is essential for students to grasp the conceptual basis underlying all the exercises. But the Kumon materials are designed to help children to learn by doing. The worksheets simply present a new idea, offer a couple of examples and sample problems, and then let the student practice the new skill through a series of introductory exercises.

In a sense, Kumon skips the long lecture about the mechanics of swimming in favor of a brief explanation and a demonstration of what it looks like, and then tells children to dive into the pool and put it to use. And as Kumon Instructors report time and again, the vast majority of children do very well. What about the few who don't get it? The Instructor is right there to offer hints, answer questions, and make problems easier to understand.

In practice, the Instructor already knows, for example, that Michael's worksheets for today's Center visit include the introduction to subtraction. She is observing Michael to see how he adapts to the new operation. If he has a question, she is right there. She patiently coaches him on the new operation, giving hints, suggestions and asking him to try some more introductory problems. If he has trouble, she may assign the same group of worksheets again until gradually he is able to do the whole set without making a mistake. When he can breeze through that set, not only getting all the problems right, but completing each sheet within the prescribed time range, she knows he's got the hang of it. Time to move on to the next batch of worksheets, some of which will present the same kind of problems as before and some of which will challenge him with slightly more difficult problems.

The idea is to 1) keep the student from getting discouraged, 2) reinforce the material just learned, and 3) develop the student's skills just a little bit more than at the previous level. In this way, the worksheets always lead the students up the "Kumon path" slowly, but always with a firm footing. Helping children to maintain confidence in their abilities even when they are faced with challenging new material is one of the strongest features of the Kumon Method. Instructors know that the real goal is not to finish X number of worksheets this month, but to develop a successful attitude that will help the student *learn how to learn.*

As we noted before, one big advantage of the Kumon materials is that they enable Instructors to identify each student's individual needs with pinpoint accuracy. Personalized help is more efficient for the Instructor and far more useful for the student when the exact problem area is known.

The same is true of the materials themselves. Unlike school textbooks, which are often merely reprinted year after year, the worksheets are completely periodically reevaluated. An international team of mathematicians and linguists who have education experience and are experts in the Kumon Method regularly get together to confer on needed revisions to the worksheets. These experts come from Australia, New Zealand, England, the U.S., Canada, Japan, Latin America and beyond to insure that Kumon's study materials are as good as they can possibly be.

Revised materials are tested in specific Centers to make sure the revisions hit the intended mark. The group then analyzes feedback from those Centers, and makes additional changes if necessary. Only when they are satisfied, are the new worksheets printed and distributed to all the Kumon Centers. This kind of fine-tuning of instructional materials is something that textbook publishers can only dream about, and it is one of the things about which Kumon is the most proud. Matt Lupsha, Vice President of Education Services for Kumon NA, insists that this process of constantly revising and improving the worksheets is emblematic of Kumon's approach because it shows the company's endless quest to provide better instruction: "Instruction is the soul of the Kumon Method. It's what

Every Child An Achiever

we do best. It's what distinguishes us from other education companies."

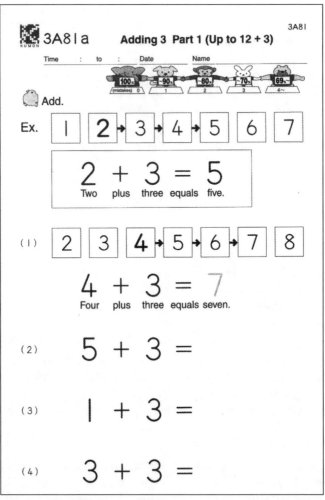

Math 3A 81a *Worksheet 3A81a is a good example of how students use the Kumon materials for independent learning. Here, students begin adding 3 to a series of one digit numbers. There are two simple example problems with number lines to illustrate that addition is an extension of counting. Note the child-friendly format: large numbers and words, simple terminology and a clear, approachable layout. Remember, prior to reaching addition in Level 3A, a child will have thoroughly mastered number facts on the first four levels of the Kumon Math materials. Addition is not introduced until a student has demonstrated the ability to read, write and count up to 220.*

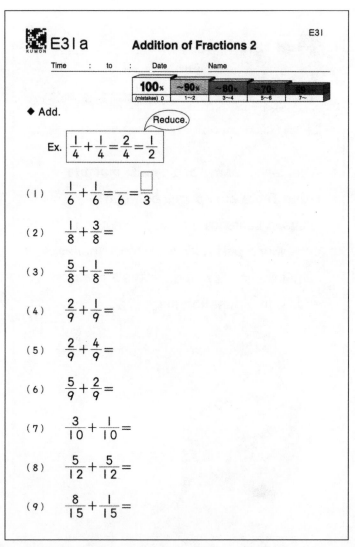

Math E 31a *Here we see how Kumon has students practice the addition of fractions using common denominators. Students are shown an example and then asked to complete similar types of problems. The focus is on the process and reducing the answer to its lowest possible terms. The addition of fractions is only introduced after students have mastered the four basic arithmetic operations – addition, subtraction, multiplication and division.*

AI 121a

Name: _____

Date: /   /

Making Short Sentences 1
Punctuation

Time: :   —   :

100%	~90%	~80%	~70%	~9%
(mistakes) 0	–	–	1	2~

I Read the sentences and circle the time taken.

A sentence always begins with a **capital letter.** There are **spaces** between the words. A sentence that tells something ends with a **period(.).** A sentence that asks something is called a question. A question ends with a **question mark (?).**

Under 15 seconds ☆☆☆	15-30 seconds ☆☆	Over 30 seconds ☆

Reading A1 121a *Like math, Kumon's Reading program focuses on developing the basic skills needed to succeed in school and beyond. This particular set of worksheets introduces some fundamental rules of English grammar and written communication. Simple exercises using each rule appear in the following pages. This set is an excerpt from Reading Level A1, one of six levels in the Sentence Building Block, which comes after the Word Building Block. After mastering all of the levels in the Sentence Building Block, a student advances to the Paragraph Building Block.*

Clauses 4   EI 31

EI 31a

Name: _____ Date: / / Time: : ~ :

100%	~90%	~80%	~70%	69%~
(mistakes) 0	1	2	3	4~

■ When reading about education, you may come across the following vocabulary words. Complete the passage using the vocabulary words defined below.

Education

academic — concerned with general education

handicap — something that limits a person mentally or physically

military — of or about armed forces or war

standard (s) — something used for judging quality

technical — of or about practical, mechanical, or industrial work, or applied science

textbook (s) — a book for regular study by pupils

From kindergarten through high school, students receive
1) _____ training in general subjects. During this training, students read all kinds of 2) _____, and must meet the academic 3) _____ of quality that their schools and teachers set for them. Students who want to work with machines after graduation may go to 4) _____ colleges. Those who want to serve in the armed forces usually go to 5) _____ academies. There are special schools for the mentally disabled, although many students with this 6) _____ are now attending regular schools.

Reading E1 31a *This excerpt from Level E1 introduces vocabulary as part of a 90-sheet section focused on learning about clauses. Exercises in this set teach students how to use specific types of descriptive words to convey information. Level E1 is a part of the Paragraph Building Block. It is succeeded by the Summary Block and then by the Critical Reading Block.*

Classrooms

There are two types of Kumon classrooms. The first is the more familiar—a child's regular school classroom. At this writing there are thousands of children using Kumon to supplement their school curriculum in public and private schools in North America. Schools using Kumon simply set aside time every day to do the Kumon worksheets. Students do their work and make corrections each day. There is usually no Kumon homework assigned.

Most students using Kumon in North America—and around the world—attend a local Kumon Math and Reading Center. A vast network of Kumon Centers has sprung up all over North America, and approximately 140,000 children are studying in these Centers today.

A Kumon Math and Reading Center might be in any number of possible locations within a community. Many of them are in shopping centers and other easily accessible commercial spaces. Others are in church annexes, community centers, and less visible locations. Regardless of the location, all Kumon Centers offer the same programs, the same teaching method, and the same opportunities for every child to grow.

Most Centers are open two afternoons a week, which is how often students attend Kumon "classes." Kumon Centers are open for a block of three hours or more, for example 3:30-6:30, to accommodate the busy schedules of children today. Based on what I've seen at dozens of Centers, an "average" Kumon day looks something like this:

Let's say you take your son to the local Kumon Center at around 3:30 on a Thursday afternoon. Perhaps you take a minute to chat with the Instructor. Then you join other parents in the waiting room while your son goes into the work area. There, he hands in his completed homework, goes to a file with his name on it, and takes out both today's worksheets and a batch of new homework the Instructor has set aside for him. Then he sits down to begin today's work. The Center is more like a study hall than a formal classroom environment. Billy can sit anywhere in the working space he likes, but he must sit down and work, not run around, talk, or disturb other children. Parents are often amazed the first time they see a

Kumon Center with 30 or 50 or 100 children working at a time, because even busy Centers are surprisingly quiet. Kumon Centers are places to study, and children are expected to come in, say hello, and sit down to do their work. Some mothers of very active younger children say this is the hardest thing for their children to get used to at first, but they do get used to it, and it doesn't take all that long. After all, there isn't anyone to play around with; the other children are there to study, too, so it becomes easier to sit down and do your own work.

The first thing he does when he starts to work is to write down his name and the starting time. Then he does the assigned number of worksheets (depending on the level of study, there are generally between 3 and 10 sheets in a day's work). When he is finished, he writes down that time and hands in his work to be graded, either by the Instructor or by a teaching assistant. While his work is being graded, he may do math or reading flashcards, read a book or challenge one of the number boards. Once again, Kumon requires that he correct any mistakes. Less than 100% correct means less than 100% mastery. The results are then entered in a special record which shows his level, the number of worksheets completed, and the time taken for every day's assignment. The Instructor looks over this chart before he goes home and chats with him for a moment as he is leaving. You stop to say good-bye to the Instructor as your son comes bounding out to greet you. Back in the car you look at your watch: it's a few minutes after 4:00. Your son has finished today's session, he's got daily homework to do for the next few days, and you're ready to go home. All in about 30 minutes.

The same basic pattern is repeated twice a week: go to the Center, hand in homework, complete that day's assignment, correct your mistakes, go home with new homework. Those two sessions of roughly 30 minutes each, plus about 15-20 minutes of homework on the other five nights a week (10 minutes for younger children) is all there is to it. No painful schedule, no arduous late-night study, no burning the midnight oil, not even as much time as it takes to watch one TV program.

In short, Kumon is not a very great time burden on either the child or the parent. And based on the many Kumon Centers I have seen around North America, almost all the parents and children enjoy coming to the Centers, talking with their friends there, and generally having a good time.

Kumon prefers to have parents grade their children's homework at home. For one thing, the child can correct mistakes immediately, and because those mistakes are corrected right away, there is much less chance that the child will repeat the same mistake. Also, many parents report that they like to see what their children are studying day by day. They don't have to rely on either the child or the Instructor for progress reports because they know precisely how well their children are doing and where they are having trouble.

Instructors

Nothing is more important to the success of the Kumon Method than having capable Instructors. Instructors not only monitor the learning process, deciding when a student is ready to move on to the next level and answering questions when a student needs help, but they also provide a very special sort of reward system for each child. So many Instructors find that just a few words of praise from them will light up a child's face, and many parents say to their Kumon Instructor, "You know, our child thinks the world of you. Everything you say makes such a big impression, we're almost jealous."

As a result, Kumon takes great care in selecting and training Instructors. Applicants who want to open a Kumon Center are qualified by a process that includes a thorough screening of their background, experience and education, as well as both written tests and interviews. If they pass the screening, a candidate Instructor must undergo intensive training that includes lectures, on-the-job training in a Center and the completion of Kumon math and reading materials. Kumon also conducts a rigorous program of continuing education for its Instructors, insisting that they attend special seminars and pass ongoing tests year after year.

If this sounds like undue "quality control," Kumon thinks differently. Without trained, dedicated, reliable people, the Kumon Method cannot succeed. It is no exaggeration to say that the Instructors in North America are among the most committed, diligent, hard-working educators in their respective communities. They care about students as individuals and that care shows in the results they help to achieve.

Unique among any type of school or learning program, Kumon students often spend year after year working and growing under the careful guidance of the same Instructor. Kumon Instructors can develop a deep awareness of the needs and strengths of individual students who remain enrolled in their Centers for 4, 5 or more years. One powerful example is Jordan Otomo of Wailuku, Hawaii, who earned a perfect score on the SAT while still a freshman in high school. Joseph worked for seven years under the adept care of Instructor Michael Ueki.

It is my observation that good parents make good Kumon Instructors. So many of the outstanding Instructors I have come across turned out to be proud mothers and fathers themselves. These are people who have extended the same love and care they felt for their own children to the students in their Centers. Once, in Canada, I was amazed to see an Instructor address dozens of her students by name. This would not be unusual in any Kumon Center, but I happened to know that this particular Instructor had over 700 students. I asked her roughly how many of their names she could remember, and she replied very matter-of-factly, "I know all their names. I remember most of their birthdays, too." Incredulous, I asked how that was possible. She said, as if it were the most obvious thing in the world, "Because they're my children."

It will probably not surprise you to learn that many Kumon parents gradually find themselves becoming more active in their local Center. Some become Center assistants, and some go on to become Instructors themselves (remember Jeannie Ianelli, the woman in Seattle at the beginning of the book? She is typical of the many people who follow the path from Kumon parent to Kumon Instructor.) Similarly, children who go through the program frequently become Kumon assistants and some of them will go on to become Instructors as well.

I said that good parents make good Kumon Instructors, but perhaps it is simpler to say that good people make good Kumon Instructors. To paraphrase Will Rogers, I've never met an Instructor I didn't like, and I think you will have the same experience. As one long-time veteran said to me, "Kumon appeals to a certain kind of person—the kind of person who loves children and believes in children and their potential. In some sense, that means that Instructors are all somewhat alike. Sure, we all look different and we're from different backgrounds, but deep down we're all basically the same kind of people."

Judging by the successes of the past few decades, those people are just what children need to make the Kumon program work spectacularly well.

It is not fair to call Kumon a job; instead, I should call it my passion. My background is in education and I took time off from teaching to explore other things. I tried many different things but found none of them fulfilling and some were downright unpleasant. Then one day by chance I was introduced to a woman who operated a Kumon Center. I asked her if she needed an assistant and she responded that she did not, but instead offered a suggestion: why didn't I contact the Kumon office about opening my own Center? I laughed at this because as a little girl I hated math, so I figured I could never run a learning center that used math. However, I did think about how much I love working with children, and I also began to think about the state of the education system in my country. So I decided to contact the local Kumon office, and the rest is history. Kumon has provided me with more satisfaction and enjoyment than any other work in my entire life. I have seen Kumon really "transform" children. I have seen children with problems in school and with low self-esteem change before my very eyes.

– Araceli Caso Barrera, Kumon Instructor, México City, México

Any time my children say, "Oh Mom, I wanna go out and play; I don't want to do my Kumon now," I just say, "OK, let's go down to the Kumon Center and tell Mrs. Paik [the Instructor] that you don't want to do Kumon anymore." And they say, "Oh, Mom, we can't do that!" So I say it's your choice, either we get the homework done and then you go play with your friends, or we go tell your Instructor that we're going to quit. And, believe me, it gets done.

– Theresa Evenson, mother, Danville, CA

Homework

One of the key principles of Kumon is that daily study must not be a burden. That is why the amount of work for each subject is calculated so that it will require no more than about 20 minutes per day. Of course, for many children any amount of homework is a "burden" because they just don't want to do it. And for parents, at least in the early weeks of Kumon study, there is sometimes a real struggle to make sure that children stick to it. This gets much better as time goes on, but only if parents are firm in the early stages. Kumon homework is not an option, not something that children do only when they feel like it or don't do because it's late or because they have soccer practice today. The earlier you train your child to do this 20 minutes of homework every day, the faster he or she will accept it. Doing Kumon becomes just one more thing that they do every day. "I tell my children it's just like brushing their teeth," says Maria Gibb, a mother in Saskatchewan, Canada. "They don't need to think about whether or not we're going to do it today; we're going to do it every day."

Here's another perspective, from Instructor Faye Komagata. Like many Instructors, Faye was a Kumon mom before opening her Center. She was convinced of the merits of doing Kumon right from the start, but she had challenges getting her children to do their homework. Faye tells her story to new parents who ask how to adapt children to doing Kumon homework daily:

> One of my sons, who was already in junior high school, had a learning disability. He had been mainstreamed and was struggling to keep up in all subject areas. He was very unhappy at school. My younger son, a sixth grader, was in and out of the gifted and talented program at his elementary school. He had considerable ability but never knew where his homework assignments were and always forgot the books he needed to bring home to do his assignments. He was always late for school, which was across the street from our house. He was popular and talented, but did not like to study or read.
>
> As you can imagine, Kumon at home was a real battle.

My sons sabotaged their work—misplacing worksheets, losing pages and leaving parts incomplete. My sister-in-law in Japan requested that I not send my younger son to Japan again with Kumon assignments to do, as he was a bad influence on her children, who were diligent in their Kumon studies. She also called me six months later to say that she had found some of his worksheets stuffed between a dresser and a wall.

I did not give up. Battle lines were drawn, and unless Kumon assignments were done, there was no TV, no soccer, no swimming, and no video games. Eventually, in the war of Mom vs. Children, Mom began to pull ahead. Not only did my children want to do things like soccer, but it also gradually became clear that Mom had an endless supply of worksheets, and that no matter how many times they were misplaced, they could always be replaced.

My children, despite all their efforts to the contrary, began to improve. They both graduated from college. My son with the learning disability received a degree in physics, while the other boy went on to graduate school. Kumon has changed their lives, not only in terms of academic achievement, but also in their self-esteem and willingness to keep trying at something until they succeed. They always seem confident that they will succeed in the end. By the way, I am still finding hidden worksheets in various areas of my house to this day...

I have heard similar stories from mothers and fathers across North America, including from several Kumon Instructors. The bottom line is very, very simple:

1) No child wants extra homework; they will naturally resist any attempt to have them adapt to any new routine; and

2) Kumon only works if you do it regularly, a little bit every day. That means children need to understand that they must do their 15-20 minutes of Kumon homework every day, week in and week out, with no compromise. In short, the parents have to lay down the law and stick to it.

Kumon is not a 2 times-a-week package. Kumon is a 7 times-a-week package with 2 Center visits.

– Sarah Strangway, Kumon Instructor, Toronto, ON

He knows that if he wants to go out and play with his friends he has to sit down and do his Kumon homework first. Sometimes he wants to see his cousins, and now they all do Kumon, too, and they'll say, "What? You didn't do your Kumon?" If he wants to play soccer or anything else, we always compare it to Kumon—if you want to do it, you have to practice, practice, practice, just like with Kumon.

– Julie Huston, mother, Kirkwood, MO

My advice to Kumon parents? Stick with it. Persist. Sure there will be fights and tantrums, but that's normal with children. Stay with it, no matter what. It really pays off.

– Nilsson Kocher, former Kumon student, now an undergraduate, Harvard University

Encouragement from parents is very important. I'm sure I would have given up if my Dad didn't keep me at it. Keep up the pressure. Your children will thank you someday.

– Roger Hong, former Kumon student, now an undergraduate, Harvard University

The children know to do their Kumon work before they ask to do something else. The children are willing to learn at an early age. If you get them started at that age, they will pick up information like a sponge. It's only later on that they discover TV and other things they'd rather be doing.

– Dr. Sunita Mathur, mother, Chesterfield, MO

My daughter does swimming, Girl Scouts, dance, violin, and acting—we go to LA for auditions and she does occasional work in TV. I don't have to tell you that she is very, very busy. But we always find time for Kumon. It just doesn't take that long.

– Laura Henry, mother, Sacramento, CA

If my children don't get their Kumon done before school, they have to come straight in after school and do it before they do anything else. Katie is doing piano, cheerleading, soccer, acting and puppetry. When people tell me they don't have time to do Kumon I always tell them that nobody is busier than my Katie is and she gets her Kumon done every day.

– Laura Bailey, mother, Tulsa, OK

There are many things that are similar to Kumon. For example, Amy is also learning piano. You have to make sure the children do it every day and they don't get in the habit of putting things off till tomorrow. It's not easy. It takes time for a child to develop a habit. They need a lot of help from their parents.

– Wei Wang, father, Chesterfield, MO

My 5-year-old is starting to realize that things come to an end. You know, like swimming lessons just ended, and soccer will be over soon. So he asked me the other day, "When is Kumon over?" And I said, "Never." And he said, "You mean, like, when I'm 16 I'm still going to be doing Kumon?" and I said "Yup." Now he's starting to get it.

I have seen other parents struggle with their children, try to do the homework in the car, then rush the children into the Kumon Center. I'm just too tired to go through all that. Believe me, with two small children, plus running a house and holding a job, I've got enough to do. So we do Kumon homework in the morning when my son is fresh and not distracted. After school, he's too tired and his friends come over and he wants to play. I don't want to have the debate about why he can't play right now because he has to do his homework. So as far as my boy is concerned, it's always breakfast, then Kumon.

– Bonnie Farias, mother, Danville, CA

The most successful children are the ones with the most supportive parents.

– Stan Laser, Kumon Instructor, Teaneck, NJ

Chapter 6

The Math Program

From their book *The Educated Child: A Parent's Guide from Preschool through Eighth Grade,* William J. Bennett, Chester E. Finn, Jr., and John T. Cribb, Jr. describe the following:

'Repetitious drill-and-kill is a waste. It just teaches rote procedures without fostering mathematical insight.'

'Too much emphasis on the mechanics of mathematics inhibits learning.'

These are the kind of comments you hear in schools where practice is considered outmoded. In such schools, children aren't as likely to get assignments that involve working a certain kind of problem several times until they master it

The real question is this: Can children get basic math skills without much practice? Or is the approach that says 'less drill and computation, more exploring and talking about math concepts' really akin to Harold Hill's 'think system' in *The Music Man*? The children of the River City band were given no instruments and no practice. Instead, Professor Hill told them if they would just 'think' the Minuet in G, someday they'd be able to play it. 'Children talk about math a lot. They write about math, but they don't actually do it,' complains a frustrated California parent. It sounds a lot like River City.

We're all for children engaging in activities designed to illuminate mathematical ideas. The problem comes when the systematic mastery of basic skills is sacrificed. Here is the reality: most children must practice math, and practice a lot, in order to learn it well. If they are going to add, subtract, multiply, divide, find the areas of circles, calculate proportions, and perform an array of other operations with speed and proficiency, they need consistent training. That means working many problems to master fundamental skills. Without such mastery, they'll have a tough time moving forward and tackling more sophisticated problems.

Regular practice, in moderation, is not what drives children away from math. What really makes them dislike and fear math is not understanding it. 'Math anxiety' arises from not being able to work problems correctly, not understanding important concepts, and not being able to get the right answer when it's your turn at the blackboard. The antidote to such anxiety is greater familiarity with math. And such familiarity comes through repeated exposure. There is no better way for children to gain confidence about working problems and tackling challenges.

(Bennett, et al, *THE EDUCATED CHILD: A Parent's Guide from Preschool through Eighth Grade*, pp.324, 325.)

Kumon and math go together naturally. As we have seen, the Kumon Method was founded almost 50 years ago by a dedicated math teacher. Toru Kumon loved the power and precision of mathematics and he knew that math, if presented properly, can be both rewarding and fun. But what he saw in his own son's school textbooks was neither rewarding nor fun nor particularly useful. He found that the textbooks were poorly organized and not likely to help students prepare to do high school math. Mr. Kumon prepared his own math program at home, seeking to devise a simple, efficient path that would provide the most effective route for all students, regardless of age or ability, to learn higher level math. As the years went by, he refined his program constantly, and the Kumon Institute that grew from his success took up the task of fine-tuning the program.

The result is what we know today as the Kumon Math program. It is without any doubt one of the most carefully designed, most well thought-out programs available anywhere to teach children to do math. And not just "do math" but truly *master* the basics of early, middle, and higher-level mathematics, step by step, right from the beginning. Kumon Math is recommended by educators as a proven way to bolster essential skills. It is featured, for example, in *The Principal's Guide to Raising Math Achievement* as one reliable approach to boosting math scores. The book notes, "Kumon Math has traditionally been taught at learning centers . . . for mathematics remediation or enrichment. Public and private schools have recently adopted the methodology." (*A Principal's Guide to Raising Math Achievement* by Elaine McEwan. Copyright © 2000. Reprinted permission of Corwin Press.)

Mr. Kumon understood that math will never seem interesting if the student has gaps in learning or weak points in comprehension. Learning math is like climbing a steep staircase: each step is essential to move up to the next, and if just one step is weak or broken, it can result in the student falling, sliding backwards, and losing confidence in his or her abilities. That leads to the "math anxiety" that so many parents talk about. Children who are not rock-solid in their understanding of basic arithmetic cannot proceed successfully to pre-algebra, and without a solid grasp of pre-algebra they cannot move on to algebra, and so on.

Author Jeanette Gadeberg describes Kumon as "an individualized program designed to help kids master the concepts of math with understanding and increased speed." She writes that "programs such as Kumon can help your daughter experience the increased confidence to forge ahead and the self-esteem that goes along with being able to keep up with the rest of the class." (*Raising Strong Daughters* by Jeanette Gadeberg. Copyright © 1995. Reprinted permission of Fairview Press.)

Kumon is designed to make learning math foolproof. Each step is tiny, but each one has been carefully checked again and again to be sure it is just the right prelude to the step that follows. If the student follows the Kumon Method diligently, he or she will climb those steps one after another, leaving no gaps in their learning and no weak points in their basic skills.

That is not to say that the Kumon Math program is the same as math taught in a regular school curriculum. Toru Kumon explained it this way:

> The goal of the Kumon Method is to foster the skills needed to master junior and high school mathematics. In order for students to steadily advance to this objective, only those problems necessary for reaching it were selected and included in the materials. Thus, Kumon doesn't encompass a bulky, wide-ranging curriculum like regular schools; content that is not directly connected to high school mathematics has been left out. Compared to school textbooks, the Kumon materials are lean and to the point.

One term you will hear used again and again with regard to Kumon Math is "mastery." Put a child in the math program at an early age (and that is relative: age 3 may be early for some, age 8 may be early for others) and encourage him or her to do it diligently for a few years. The result is unequivocal: that student will master the basics of math, usually at a level significantly above his or her peers in regular school—a place where the term "mastery" is seldom heard.

How can Kumon be so confident about these results?

The answer is simple: 50 years of experience and over 14 million students prove the point. Children who do Kumon Math learn math right, learn it quickly, and learn it thoroughly. Students, parents and teachers all recognize what this kind of thorough, step-by-step approach to math can achieve.

Students

Steve: *Kumon has really helped me a lot. Children used to call me "the human calculator" in school. I didn't mind that; I always thought of it as a compliment. The teacher would assign math homework at the start of class, and by the time class was over I'd have it done.*

Terry: *That's right. I remember in 4th Grade, the teacher used to compete with me doing multiplication problems using a calculator. I always beat her.*

– Steve and Terry Chu, age 16 & 15, Sacramento, CA

Kumon really helped me to develop problem-solving ability. The first part of the Kumon Math program focuses on calculation, and that is a necessary step in getting the foundations down. After that, starting in Level H, you really have to think about how you're going to solve the problem. I found that transition difficult myself, and having worked as an assistant in a Kumon Center for years now, I see other students in the same situation. Of course, the irony is that many students want to stop around Levels H and I because it gets harder, but that's actually when they're starting to learn to think.

– Roger Hong, who began Kumon at age 5 in Taiwan, moved to Canada, where he had to do it in another language, and still finished the entire math program while in junior high school. Roger scored a perfect 800 on his math SAT and is now a student at Harvard.

Teachers

Students are acquiring math facts in a concrete way which will be the basis for all math they do throughout their school careers. Kumon allows teachers to individualize in their classrooms so that each student is working at his or her own level and acquiring the skills needed to move forward. Kumon is head and shoulders above any other math program I have seen in my years as a teacher, particularly in what students gain in terms of the knowledge and confidence needed to be great math students throughout their academic careers.

– Marti Sudduth, Assistant Director, University School, Tulsa, OK

I have been using Kumon in school for approximately nine years. I feel Kumon has strengthened my students in all areas of math. Their math test scores have really increased. I believe Kumon is self-motivating and the students love it. I would encourage any teacher to use it.

– Zana Horn, Teacher,
Sumiton Elementary/Middle School, Sumiton, AL

Parents

I've always said that Kumon is the Vince Lombardi of math—just blocking and tackling every day, day in and day out.

– Michael Gordon, father, Maryland Heights, MO

My granddaughter was having problems in math and one of my church members told me about Kumon. She started in the 6th grade, now she's in 9th grade. It's really helped her math skills. Her grades have really improved. It took about a year. Several times I thought we're not really making progress because she had to go back and repeat some sections, and there were times I thought maybe we should give up. But after a year or so we saw a big difference. Now all the 9th graders are doing pre-algebra, while she's doing algebra. And she used to hate math. Now it's her favorite subject.

– Lauretta Gattison, grandmother, Oakland, CA

I think math is the most important thing, because you need it in so many things, in anything you do, whether you go to college or not. I don't want my children to struggle with math like I did. My children didn't get a math gene, because I don't have one. Before Kumon, both my children had a lot of math anxiety. They did not like math. I had to sit with them every night and help them with their math homework. I remembered that so well from my own childhood, and I didn't want that for my children. So I looked at all the different supplemental education systems. I especially liked the repetition that Kumon provided. I think math is like building blocks. If you don't get each block in order, you don't get math. You have to have those sequential steps, and Kumon provides those steps. Now my children can do their multiplication faster than anybody. My son's teachers can't believe it. He can do fractions much faster than I can; I usually get it, but it takes a while.

– Kerri Niday, mother, Danville, CA

After the recent acts of terrorism, the principal of our elementary school decided there should be some way for every child to do to something to help. So the school ran a fund-raising drive and asked the children to bring in whatever amount they wanted to for donations. Of course, every child, especially the ones in kinder- garten, went right to their parents and asked for money to donate.

My children never thought to ask us. They went into their own wallets and got their own money. That afternoon someone from the school called to inform me that my daughter[in kinder- garten] had just brought in $105 and asked if I knew about it and did I really want this sum to go to the donation fund? I told them I didn't know anything about it, which was true. The school was obviously very concerned. They said, "Karen came to school with over $100, and she didn't even tell you, and, well, maybe she doesn't understand what this means..."

I said, "She understands exactly *what it means. Karen is in Kumon. She understands quantity and numbers very well, believe me. She understands that she had a total of $117. And she has an appreciation for that amount because she earns it at the rate of $2 a week. It was her life savings. Of that, she donated $105. So, she's not a perfect angel; she didn't give every penny, she saved some for herself. But she gave until it hurt because she wanted to help."*

Still, I could sense that they were really concerned that a child in kindergarten couldn't possibly grasp the concept of big numbers like that. Later we found out that for each dollar donated they taped a small American flag up in the school hallway. They put 105 flags up there so Karen could have a better appreciation for such a big number. That was really very kind of them—but also totally unnecessary because, thanks to Kumon, she understands numbers and arithmetic perfectly well.

– Susan Figenshau, mother, St. Louis, MO

We started the program a year ago. Meghan was struggling in school with everything. She was developmentally about a year behind everyone else. Kumon is really helping things along. When we started Kumon, she was just going into second grade, and she had to think real hard about problems like 2 + 1. Gradually, by doing the worksheets every day, she improved. There were periods when it was a real struggle, and then she'd break through and get it, and then another little struggle, and then the breakthrough. I didn't even really see how far she had come. Then she started third grade. At the beginning of each school year, I'm always wor- rying, wondering, 'Are we going to make it all right this year...?'

Then one day she came home and didn't say anything right away. I think it was about 6 o'clock, and she'd been home for three hours, and she said just as casual as can be, "Oh, I have a surprise, Mom." And she takes out this certificate from her backpack that says "Math Facts Whiz Child." I was amazed. My daughter? She tells me that when she came in from lunch the teacher had put it on her desk. They had all done 100 Math Facts and set the timer for 3 minutes and she was the only one in the whole class who finished them all. And she got 100%.

I went into the bathroom and cried my eyes out. I mean, this is the first success she's had since she started school. And she had only been in Kumon for about one year at that point.

Then they did the same kind of test for subtraction, and she did it again! Same thing. That was a few weeks ago. Now she gets to walk around and hand everybody their papers, set the timers, and then go play with the computers. All the children ask her what's her secret, but she says, "I don't want them to know my secret!" She understands that Kumon has given her an edge.

– Mary Beth Smith, mother, Tulsa, OK

5A 147a *Enjoyable maze-type exercises gradually teach young children the shape and stroke order for numbers.*

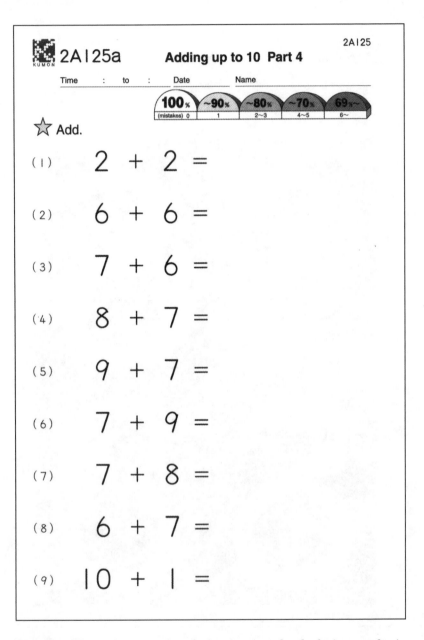

2A125a   Adding up to 10 Part 4

Time   :   to   :   Date   Name

100%	~90%	~80%	~70%	69%~
(mistakes) 0	1	2~3	4~5	6~

☆ Add.

(1)   2 + 2 =

(2)   6 + 6 =

(3)   7 + 6 =

(4)   8 + 7 =

(5)   9 + 7 =

(6)   7 + 9 =

(7)   7 + 8 =

(8)   6 + 7 =

(9)   10 + 1 =

2A 125a *Kumon's strong foundation in mental calculation results in students answering questions such as these instantly.*

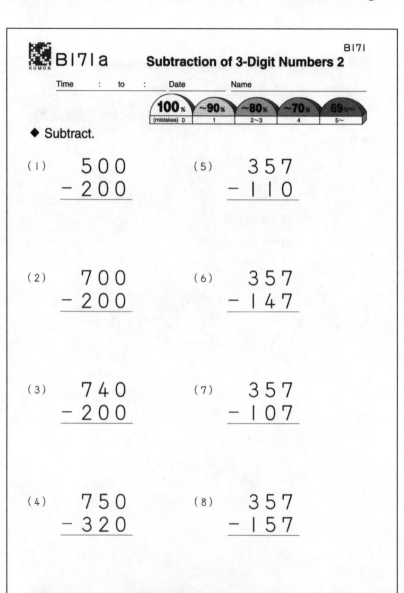

KUMON B171a **Subtraction of 3-Digit Numbers 2**

Time : to : Date Name

100%	~90%	~80%	~70%	69%~
(mistakes) 0	1	2~3	4	5~

◆ Subtract.

```
(1)    5 0 0        (5)    3 5 7
     - 2 0 0             - 1 1 0


(2)    7 0 0        (6)    3 5 7
     - 2 0 0             - 1 4 7


(3)    7 4 0        (7)    3 5 7
     - 2 0 0             - 1 0 7


(4)    7 5 0        (8)    3 5 7
     - 3 2 0             - 1 5 7
```

Have you been practicing the multiplication tables?

B 171a *With a solid foundation of mental calculation skills, Kumon students aim to complete these questions quickly and without writing carryovers.*

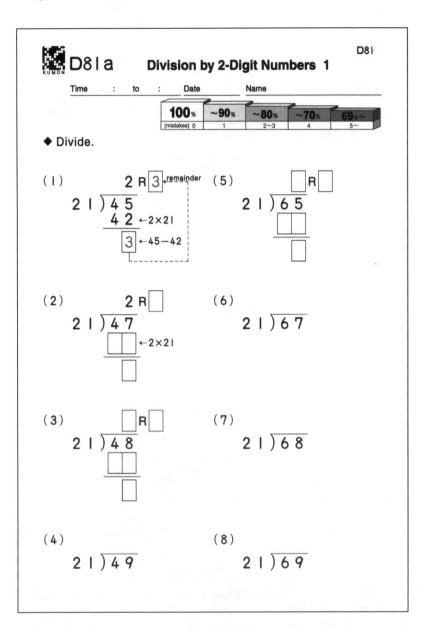

D81a

D81a Division by 2-Digit Numbers 1

Time : to : Date Name

100%	~90%	~80%	~70%	69%~
(mistakes) 0	1	2~3	4	5~

◆ Divide.

(1)
```
              2 R 3 ←remainder
   2 1 ) 4 5
         4 2   ←2×21
           3   ←45−42
```

(5)
```
              □ R □
   2 1 ) 6 5
         □□
          □
```

(2)
```
              2 R □
   2 1 ) 4 7
         □□   ←2×21
          □
```

(6)
```
   2 1 ) 6 7
```

(3)
```
              □ R □
   2 1 ) 4 8
         □□
          □
```

(7)
```
   2 1 ) 6 8
```

(4)
```
   2 1 ) 4 9
```

(8)
```
   2 1 ) 6 9
```

D 81a *Students are introduced to long division with an already completed question and hints, followed by a series of partially completed questions. Note how the first questions increase in difficulty in very small increments.*

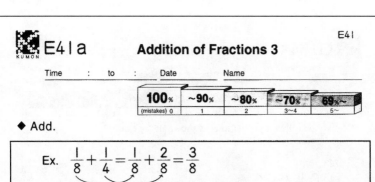

E4I

E4ㅣa   **Addition of Fractions 3**

Time   :   to   :   Date   Name

100%	~90%	~80%	~70%	69%~
(mistakes) 0	1	2	3~4	5~

◆ Add.

Ex. $\dfrac{1}{8}+\dfrac{1}{4}=\dfrac{1}{8}+\dfrac{2}{8}=\dfrac{3}{8}$

When adding fractions, rewrite the fractions so that the denominators are equal.

(1) $\dfrac{3}{8}+\dfrac{1}{4}=\dfrac{3}{8}+\dfrac{\square}{8}=$

(2) $\dfrac{5}{8}+\dfrac{1}{4}=$

(3) $\dfrac{1}{8}+\dfrac{1}{2}=\dfrac{1}{8}+\dfrac{\square}{8}=$

(4) $\dfrac{3}{8}+\dfrac{1}{2}=$

(5) $\dfrac{1}{10}+\dfrac{1}{5}=$

(6) $\dfrac{7}{10}+\dfrac{1}{5}=$

(7) $\dfrac{1}{8}+\dfrac{3}{4}=$

E 41a *This page, adding fractions with different denominators, illustrates how Kumon uses examples and partially completed questions to guide students in new concepts.*

Every Child An Achiever

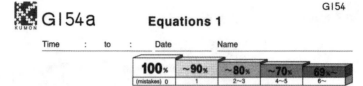

G154a　　　Equations 1

Time　　:　to　:　Date　　　Name

100%	~90%	~80%	~70%	69%~
(mistakes) 0	1	2~3	4~5	6~

◆ Solve the following equations as shown in the examples.

Ex.

$$2x = 6$$

[Sol] $x = 6 \times \dfrac{1}{2}$

$$x = 3$$

To change the equation into the form 'x = a number' we need to transform '$2x$' to 'x'. We do this by multiplying both sides of the equation by '$\dfrac{1}{2}$'.

$$-\frac{1}{3}x = -\frac{5}{6}$$

[Sol] $x = -\dfrac{5}{6} \times (-3)$

$$x = \frac{5}{2}$$

To transform '$-\dfrac{1}{3}x$' to 'x', multiply both sides by '-3'.

(1) $-3x = 2$

[Sol]　$x = 2 \times \left(-\dfrac{1}{\boxed{}} \right)$

　　　$x =$

(2) $-5x = -\dfrac{5}{6}$

(3) $2x = -\dfrac{2}{5}$

(4) $5x = \dfrac{3}{4}$

(5) $\dfrac{1}{3}x = -\dfrac{1}{5}$

[Sol]　$x = -\dfrac{1}{5} \times \boxed{}$

　　　$x =$

(6) $-\dfrac{x}{5} = \dfrac{3}{10}$

(7) $-\dfrac{1}{2}x = -\dfrac{2}{3}$

(8) $\dfrac{x}{21} = \dfrac{2}{7}$

G 154a *As students advance into algebra, the examples and explanations become more detailed.*

J 116 a Quadratic Equations and Complex Numbers

Time : to : Date Name

100%	90%	80%	70%	69%~
(mistakes) 0	–	1	2	3~

Quadratic Formula I

When $ax^2 + bx + c = 0$
$$x = \frac{-b \pm \sqrt{b^2 - 4ac}}{2a}$$

Quadratic Formula II

When $ax^2 + 2b'x + c = 0$
$$x = \frac{-b' \pm \sqrt{b'^2 - ac}}{a}$$

Ex.
$$3x^2 + 5x - 7 = 0$$
$$x = \frac{-5 \pm \sqrt{25 - 4 \cdot 3 \cdot (-7)}}{6}$$
$$= \frac{-5 \pm \sqrt{109}}{6}$$

Ex.
$$5x^2 - 8x + 4 = 0$$
$$x = \frac{4 \pm \sqrt{16 - 20}}{5}$$
$$= \frac{4 \pm \sqrt{-4}}{5}$$
Substitute $\sqrt{-4} = 2i$
$$= \frac{4 \pm 2i}{5}$$

Solve the following equations by applying the quadratic formulas.

(1) $2x^2 + 5x + 4 = 0$

(2) $4x^2 - 4x + 5 = 0$

When the solution of an equation is an imaginary number, we call it an
imaginary root, or a complex number solution.

J 116a *Students learn the Quadratic Formulae.*

Chapter 7

The Reading Program

Most likely everyone who has ever heard of Kumon knows about its success with the teaching of math. Particularly in North America, where there was hardly a reading program to speak of just a decade ago, the expression "Kumon Math" was practically synonymous with Kumon itself. That was years ago. Since then Kumon has developed a first-rate reading program in North America. Today, the system is known in most places as "Kumon Math and Reading," as you will likely notice from the sign on your local Kumon Center or any written materials you may have received there. Reading and math share equal billing today, and the number of reading program students is growing rapidly, on track to catch up to the math program enrollment some years down the road.

The reading program is not an add-on or an afterthought. Reading and language programs have been an integral part of the Kumon Method in Japan for decades. It just took a little while to develop a really strong, well-designed reading program in North America that is a perfect complement to the math program.

First, just to give you an idea of how far back the idea of a reading program goes in the Kumon philosophy, the following comments reflect the importance of reading from a famous mathematician, none other than Toru Kumon himself:

> From the beginning, one of the important goals of the Kumon Method has always been to nurture children who enjoy reading books. Since I happened to be a teacher of mathematics, our Center expansion initially took place with mathematics. However, my first goal of home education was increasing my child's vocabulary and instilling in him a love of reading.

> In order to raise children with high abilities, it is essential that we help them to acquire ample vocabularies and an advanced level of reading. Reading books to children is also an indispensable process in fostering children who will enjoy reading by themselves. Parents should begin reading as many books as possible to children as early as possible.

> We should recognize that language is the foundation of all abilities. We should also keep in mind that speaking and reading abilities are fostered through proper approaches in early childhood, preferably starting right after birth. It goes without saying that the benefits described above can be realized only when a "just right" level of material, appropriate to the child's own level of development, is given.

> Through language education and abundant reading experiences, our children come to know that they are surrounded by all kinds of different words, people and ideas. Furthermore, reading books provides children with opportunities to think for themselves, come to know themselves, and broaden their own horizons. Such well-read children will eventually grow into the type of people who are capable of living happy, productive lives and actively striving to help make the world a better place. These are the kind of people we will need in the 21st century, and it is our mission at Kumon to nurture these talents in as many students as possible.

Did you catch that? "My first goal . . . was increasing my

child's vocabulary and instilling in him a love of reading" and ". . . language is the foundation of all abilities." Quite a pronouncement from a math teacher! So much for reading being an afterthought. Toru Kumon himself acknowledged just how important it is for young children to develop strong reading skills. Reading, he points out, not only helps children do their schoolwork, but also to "think for themselves, come to know themselves, and broaden their own horizons." That is a very potent message for parents in any age.

Kumon's Reading program began in Japan as a way for Japanese speakers to learn English. Later on, there developed a popular program to teach Japanese children to read fluently in their own language. Later still, in Australia, a reading program for native English speakers emerged. Despite its earlier incarnations, the reading program that exists today is unique to North America, and it is by far the most highly developed program of its kind. It is designed to help native speakers improve their reading comprehension, regardless of age or ability. The fundamental goal is to allow students to develop the reading comprehension of a high school student, much as the math program was designed to allow children to do high school-level math.

The reading program materials look just like those for the math program—200 two-sided worksheets per level, although the sheets contain words, sentences, short stories, and passages from world literature. As of this writing, the reading program consists of 22 Levels, from 7A to K. If your addition is faster than mine, you have already noticed that the numbers don't add up: somebody must have stuck some extra levels in there. And that's exactly what has happened. Unlike the math program, there are extra levels added from A through E. Thus, after AI, there is AII, then BI and BII, CI and CII, up through Level EI and EII.

This augmentation of the reading levels will probably keep expanding, as Lisa Kaul, an executive with Kumon's Materials Development Department, explains:

> We decided it was important to have less repetition in
> the reading program. It makes good sense to repeat
> math problems again and again, but re-reading pas-

sages from literature more than a few times is likely to turn off the student rather than lead to mastery of a problem the way it does in math. For this reason, we have added several new sections in the middle Levels— the 'Twos'—and the response has been very positive. By doubling the number of worksheets in these levels, we can get the same benefits of repeating work at a certain stage of learning without actually having students read the same passages over and over again. Like everything in Kumon, the student data [i.e., the results observed from working with tens of thousands of children] are critically important. Just as in the math program, we study the data, look for problems in the worksheets, places where children are having trouble, and we fix them. We would never say the system is perfect, but I can guarantee it gets better with each revision.

An interesting feature shared by both the reading and math programs is the emphasis to work quickly and carefully. Of course, the reading program has its own Standard Completion Time range, but it is quite generous. While this is important for teaching proper reading comprehension skills, it may also have had an unintended side benefit for children who are learning much more than just improved comprehension.

As I noted above, the reading program was specifically designed to help English-speaking children to increase their reading comprehension, and Kumon does not market the program for any other purpose. At the same time, Kumon acknowledges that some Centers and some parents in various Centers do employ the reading program as a means of teaching English to students with limited English proficiency with much success. Once again, this is not official Kumon policy and no claims are made for this kind of study (just as no claims are made for using Kumon with learning disabled children), but the results speak for themselves. Which is why more and more parents are turning to Kumon to help their children learn or improve their English.

The first time I noticed this was when I was visiting some outstanding Kumon Centers in Hawaii. I met a lot of bright, wonderful children, and many of the children were the sons and daughters of recent Asian immigrants. I couldn't help but notice a very cute little girl at the next table. She zipped through her worksheets for that day and was chattering away to her friends while at the same time helping her little sister do her own Kumon. The Instructor saw me notice her and smiled. "That's Annie Mei," she said. "Her Mom is Chinese, doesn't speak a word of English. About a year ago she brought Annie to our Center and asked to put her in the reading program. Of course, the mother can't read English herself, so she cannot correct the homework, which posed some special challenges. But I agreed anyway."

"When Annie first came here a year ago she was so quiet, so shy, you would not believe it. She never spoke a word. Now look at her." I was looking. Maybe 7 years old, she hadn't stopped talking for at least the past half hour and seemed to be carrying on at least two conversations at once in very fluent English. "She's a little chatterbox," I said, and the Instructor laughed. "Yes, you could say she's picked up the language. In fact, she's going through the Levels even faster than some of the children who are native speakers. That's her sister Lilly next to her. Lilly is in kindergarten now, and she's joined us, too. The two of them are quite a pair of success stories."

Two days later I heard about another child, a Korean boy with zero English vocabulary named Jeeseok Kim. He charged into the Kumon Reading program in the 3rd grade, doing double the normal amount of homework every night. His Instructor told me, "The normal time for someone his age to go through an ESL [English as a Second Language] course is 14 months. He did it in 8. Not only that, but when I first met him he used to come to class like a turtle, head down, very meek. Now he stands up straight and proud and he speaks up in clear English." Again, all the credit cannot go to Kumon, and yet, it can't all go to television either. In fact, Jeeseok's mom said, "Whenever I am asked how he could graduate from an ESL class after only eight months in the States, I say that the Kumon Reading program really helped his English a lot."

In Miami I visited what is very likely the most "international" Center in Kumon North America. The parents come from places like Argentina, Brazil, Venezuela, Colombia, Cuba,

Honduras, Ecuador, and Panama, as well as Spain, Portugal, Italy, Greece and half a dozen other countries ("We're a little United Nations here," explains Instructor Angela Onde). But the children all have one thing in common—they are all living in America now and they need to read, write and speak English well if they are to get ahead. A large percentage of the parents at this Center have put their children in the reading program expressly to help with their English studies.

"Most of the parents came to Miami not long ago from another country," Angela explains, "and they are choosing Kumon as the 'gateway' to supplement their children's regular American schooling and to reinforce their English." I met a first grader from Venezuela named Viviana Arguello who had only been in the U.S. about one year. Viviana helped to translate for her Mom, who explained that in their short time doing Kumon they already could see improvement in her English ability. "She reads street signs all the time when we are driving," her mother explained, "And she's already bringing home A's on her report card. We are very happy."

Octavio Goren, an 11-year-old from Argentina, also impressed me. He has only been in the U.S. for a few years. His older siblings got a head start on learning the new language, but his mother says he could not speak English at all. She put him in Kumon a little over a year ago to help with his language learning. Now she says he is the one who translates for her, not the older children. "People are very impressed with his English," she says, "His school class is held in both Spanish and English but his teacher wants him to move to a regular all-English class."

What is in the Reading Program?

The program starts at a very simple level, where students look at words and sentences on their worksheets, hear them being pronounced correctly on an accompanying CD, and practice repeating what they hear. This helps to build phonemic awareness or recognition that words are made up of letters and sounds. This leads to what is called a "sight word" vocabulary, or words that a child has learned to recognize on sight and pronounce from habit, even though he or she may have no idea how to pronounce the component parts of those words. Academics who study language learning call this approach "whole language" study.

As the program progresses, students learn the sounds of individual letters and letter combinations, what is known as "phonics." Educators are still divided over the relative merits of whole language vs. phonics as the ideal approach to teaching reading. Kumon, as you might expect, does not claim that one is right and the other wrong, but sees valid points in both approaches. Thus, the reading program uses both methods and applies them in a comprehensive approach that its own studies have shown to be most effective.

In addition to learning to recognize and sound out words, students develop fine motor skills and learn to write clearly with a pencil, to trace letters and words, and then to write the answers to word questions. In addition, there is a lot of oral work at the earlier levels. Students read aloud to their Instructor, which provides an opportunity to correct pronunciation and check on understanding. From there, as they develop sentence-building skills, they learn to identify sentence topics, ideas and types of language, and later on, to understand paragraphs, to reason, summarize, and critique an author's main point, to separate fact from opinion, and even to argue and persuade in English. Each skill level adds new vocabulary and reviews words introduced at earlier levels. Timed reading passages are included for building reading fluency. Comprehension questions are used to develop critical thinking skills.

Because the Kumon Math program devotes a great deal of time to practicing basic arithmetic and mathematical functions, many people expect the reading program will have unit after unit of grammar drills. In fact, Kumon spends relatively little time practicing grammar in the way we parents remember it from school. Instead, Kumon looks at language as an organic thing, words as part of sentences and sentences as part of paragraphs, and so on. Of course, students learn grammar, and they must understand it, but the main thrust of the reading program is to learn to be a good reader, to understand what one reads and to be able to read intelligently, analytically and critically. These are precisely the skills that will be important in high school and even more essential in college and beyond.

To further hone reading skills, the materials have excerpts from fiction and non-fiction. These exercises not only extend the love of reading but enhance knowledge of subject areas such as science, social studies and geography.

In addition to the worksheets, Kumon offers a Recommended reading List. For each level, from 7A to I, there are at least 15 books recommended for students to supplement and strengthen the reading skills they are developing in the program. Needless to say, Kumon has spent a great deal of time examining literature to find what is most appropriate for each level of study and appropriate for children of all ages to be reading. Kumon also stresses the benefits of oral reading, both in class and at home. Beginning readers should practice reading aloud at home, and parents should encourage that. Mr. Kumon often emphasized the importance of reading aloud to even the very youngest children. Once they get older and are beginning to read for themselves, let them do the oral reading.

When Alex started Kumon, I was saying, "I don't know if this is right for us," and within 2 weeks he knew all the phonetics for every letter and started reading words, and I said, "WOW!" Now he's in kindergarten and he reads chapter books. He reads a story every night. In school, they're still tracing. I mean it. They are tracing the letter A, drawing the little a.

– Theresa Evenson, mother, Danville, CA

We have a reading club in the library every summer. They encourage children to read. If you read 25 books, they give you a small gift, if you read 50 they give you a certificate for ice cream. I read 200 books.

– Jeffrey Chien, age 7, Livingston, NJ

He reads to his baby brother every day, one book a day, and he corrects my English all the time. He is teaching me how to read English. He makes me pronounce things over and over. He makes me repeat. Where did he learn that, do you think?

– Jeffrey's mom, Livingston, NJ

He is so good at reading; he just reads sentences like an adult reading sentences. Children in his Kindergarten class are still sounding out letters.

– Bonnie Farias, mother, Danville, CA

My 2nd grader was having trouble, really struggling with reading. [After we started Kumon,] the first thing I noticed was a change in confidence in reading. She was very nervous about reading out loud before, when she was called on at school, they would have to read just a couple of sentences but she never raised her hand; now she raises her hand all the time, she reads aloud at church. Things have really changed.

– Gayle Hantak, mother, St. Louis, MO

I expected the reading program to be all right, not great but just so-so. Now I have to tell you that I am very impressed with the quality of the literature. My daughter hasn't just improved her reading ability; she's also learned all about different religions, the galaxy and various constellations, different ways of life, cultural traditions, geography, and so on. That, plus the comprehension training is a big, big help with many school subjects.

– Maria Gibb, mother, Saskatoon, SK

One thing I really love about the way that Kumon presents reading is the different ways they do it—crossword puzzles, complete the sentence games, etc. Lots of variety means that children look forward to turning the page. With math there's not much they can do to make the drills interesting, but with reading they can do a lot and they do. I think every child should learn how to read this way.

– Julie Huston, mother, Kirkwood, MO

6A 99b

🎧 Let's say the words. Find them in the picture.

five bananas

one full cup

seven funny clowns

6A 99b *Kumon's learning-to-read levels are filled with colorful artwork and enjoyable exercises to make the reading process appealing for young students.*

3A 1

3A 1a

Name : _____

Spelling Patterns 1

Date :   /   /

Time :   :   —   :

🦆 Paying attention to the a r sound, read each word aloud before tracing and writing the letters.

c a r

car

st a r

st

guit a r

guit

3A 1a *Kumon exposes students to phonics as part of the learning-to-read process. By tracing words and filling in missing letters as they read, students also learn the connection between sound and spelling.*

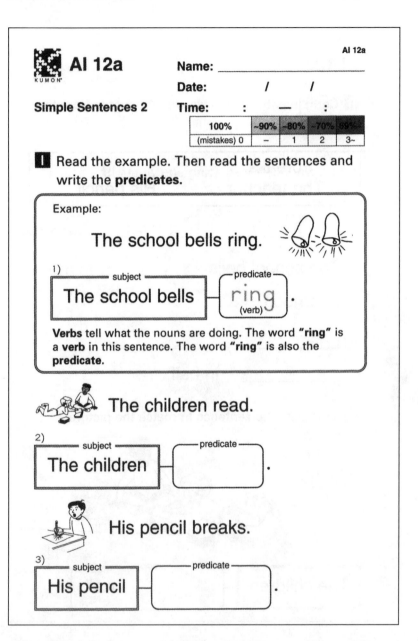

AI 12a

Name: _____

Date: / /

Simple Sentences 2

Time: : — :

100%	~90%	~80%	~70%	69%~
(mistakes) 0	–	1	2	3~

1 Read the example. Then read the sentences and write the **predicates**.

Example:

The school bells ring.

1)
subject — The school bells
predicate — ring (verb) .

Verbs tell what the nouns are doing. The word **"ring"** is a **verb** in this sentence. The word **"ring"** is also the **predicate**.

The children read.

2)
subject — The children
predicate — .

His pencil breaks.

3)
subject — His pencil
predicate — .

AI 12a *Though the goal of the Kumon Reading program is improved reading comprehension, certain sections, such as this exercise from the "Sentence Building Block," focus on key grammar skills. As in the math program, explanations and examples always accompany new concepts.*

CII 80a

CII 80a

KUMON®

Organizing
Information 2
Carlos and the Skunk

Name: _____

Date: /   /

Time: :   —   :

100%	~90%	~80%	~70%	69%~
(mistakes) 0	–	1	2	3~

1 Continue reading the story and then choose a title
from the shaded box that matches each chart.

> The smell from his shoes, which he had forgotten to
> clean after being sprayed by Dos Dedos, was spreading
> through the heating ducts to the entire church.
>   "Papá, I think we better go home," whispered Carlos,
> hoping no one would realize he was the source of the
> terrible smell.
>   Several families began heading for the door.
> The priest dismissed the service early.
>   Embarrassed, Carlos pushed his
> way out of the church.

1)

i. sprayed by a skunk

ii. forgetting to clean his
shoes

iii. the smell spreading
through the heating
ducts

2)

i. families headed for
the door

ii. services were
dismissed early

iii. Carlos was
embarrassed

The Cause of the Smell   The Result of the Smell
The Result of the Choir Singing   The Cause of the Service

CII 80a *Kumon students hone their reading comprehension skills
through exposure to literature from all over the world. This "Organizing
Information" section helps students understand how even fiction can be
organized into a chart format for easier interpretation.*

EI 149b

II Read each diagram and the passage, and then complete the passage according to the diagram.

Relationship between products and costs

Only a few products are made

Retail cost of each item is usually high

$$$

Many products are made

Retail cost of each item is usually lower

$

If there were only one light bulb for sale in the store, you can bet that it would be very expensive. When 1) _____ _____, and everybody wants one, the 2) _____ _____. Fortunately, light bulbs are one of the many products that are mass-produced.

For industries, starting a factory that mass-produces goods requires a large amount of capital in the form of expensive equipment. However, for the consumer, the 3)_____ _____ when 4) _____. A low retail cost is necessary for companies to stay competitive.

EI 149b *A peripheral benefit of the Kumon Reading program is an increase in students' general knowledge of the world. While the focus of this exercise is on taking information from a chart and restating it in a paragraph format, students also learn about the relationship between production volume and cost.*

H 5a

Fact and Opinion 1
Exercise

Name :

Date :   /   /   Time :   :   ~   :

100%	~90%	~80%	~70%	69%~
(mistakes) 0	–	1	2	3~

█1█ Insert one sentence part from each box into the sentence that precedes it in order to make the sentence either a fact or an opinion.

1) Fact:

South Korea is a country _____ .

> whose people are kind / bordered by North Korea

2) Fact:

The Berlin Wall _____

_____ .

> was torn down in 1989 / was the greatest symbol of the cold war

3) Opinion:

Hats _____ .

> shade the head / are very fashionable

4) Opinion:

The flag of Kenya _____

_____ .

> has a shield and two spears on it / is exquisite

H 5a *An important component of reading comprehension, especially when interpreting persuasive writing and arguments, is the ability to quickly distinguish between fact and opinion.*

K 63b

II Read the passage and mark the statement which best describes the atmosphere of the passage.

MARCELLUS

'Tis gone and will not answer.

BERNARDO

How now, Horatio? You tremble and look pale.

Is not this something more than fantasy?

What think you on't?

HORATIO

Before my God, I might not this believe

Without the sensible and true avouch

Of mine own eyes.

MARCELLUS   Is it not like the king?

HORATIO

As thou art to thyself.

Such was the very armor he had on

When he th' ambitious Norway[1] combated.

So frowned he once when, in an angry parle,[2]

He smote the sledded Polacks on the ice.

'Tis strange.

MARCELLUS

Thus twice before, and jump[3] at this dead hour,

With martial stalk hath he gone by our watch.

1. *Norway* King of Norway   2. *parle* parley
3. *jump* just, exactly

☐ Horatio induces a sense of calm and rationality.

☐ A feeling of shock and bewilderment pervades the scene after the ghost exits.

☐ There is a feeling of great excitement over the return of the ghost.

K 63b *In the higher levels of the Kumon Reading program, students read advanced texts, such as this excerpt from Shakespeare's* Macbeth, *and learn about literary devices such as plot, atmosphere and irony.*

Chapter 8

Does it Really Work?

This is perhaps the easiest question to answer for yourself. All you need to do is talk to some parents at your local Kumon Center. I can tell you that it works, and the Kumon people can tell you that it works, but that should not persuade you. Go talk to some other parents who, like yourself, came to Kumon with questions and doubts, decided to give it a try and are now in a position to judge the results for themselves.

There is only one point to keep in mind, and that is the period of time it takes to see results. Of course, there are parents who will swear that they have seen positive results in their children after only two weeks. That is heartening to hear, but those are exceptional cases. Many parents say they begin to see results after roughly six months. That is a bit more common. However, when I interviewed people all over North America, the vast majority said that it usually takes about nine months to a year for most students to reach their equivalent school math or reading, and then the results really take off. More than a dozen people in different cities said to me in almost exactly the same words: "It took us about a year, and then—click!—everything fell into place."

In other words, a child who has been doing Kumon for close

to a year is going to exhibit clear, unmistakable signs of all the positive attributes the Kumon Method produces. Specifically, after 9-12 months in the program, you should expect to see visible improvement in the subject of study (math or reading), plus improvements in other important areas: self-confidence, self-esteem, study habits, concentration, etc. These are attributes that the Kumon Method has cultivated in millions of children worldwide over the years, and the Kumon people are completely confident that you will see the same results in your own child.

For this reason, it is important to talk to parents who have some experience with Kumon over this minimum time period. Parents who have only been involved in the program for a month or so may be ecstatic about it or they may be wondering if it will truly pay off as they have heard it will. Like them, you need to talk to people who can speak from experience about what Kumon can do for any child if you just give it a little time.

Kumon is Not a Quick Fix

This brings up an important point. Many parents come to Kumon in search of remedial help with math or reading or both. This is fine; Kumon is remarkably effective in finding the gaps in a child's understanding of either subject and filling in the foundations so they are rock-solid. From there a child can progress surprisingly quickly through more advanced levels, so that a student who started out needing remedial help because he or she was a year behind his/her class soon winds up studying a year ahead of normal grade level. This happens all the time.

However, some parents are not looking for such a thorough solution. They hear, for example, that Kumon teaches math better than anyone, and they want their child to get a quick "shot in the arm" in math to help finish a course, pass a test, or whatever. Then they plan to stop Kumon and coast on the short-term benefits for a while.

I have heard many Instructors make the same complaint: "Parents come to my Center and say that their son or daughter has a big math test next term and they want to do a 'crash course' to ensure that the child aces the test. I have to tell them it just doesn't work like that."

Kumon is not a "cram school." Kumon is not the thing you do the night before a test or the week before a test or even a couple of months before a test. As you have already seen, the Kumon Method was designed to allow children to build a very solid foundation in math or reading, and then develop at their own pace, and develop fully so as to master that subject completely. Kumon is not a magic potion; it is not, unfortunately, "a pill you take to get smarter," as one child gleefully explained Kumon to me. The bottom line is that Kumon requires hard work and patience. What it promises in return is The Big Payoff:

- **A strong academic footing**, not just for the next test or report card, but for the rest of your life;
- **Confidence** in your ability to learn and overcome obstacles in learning; and
- **Good study habits** (read: self-discipline) that will serve you well throughout your life.

William Murphy and Philip Smith were just settling in to life as roommates at Morehouse College in Atlanta, Georgia, when they discovered that Kumon had played a role in both of their journeys to the school. "Kumon is the reason I was able to do so well on the SAT and get into Morehouse," Philip said adding that his father, a former NBA player, always stressed academics at home. William credits Kumon with helping him to "see problems more easily" and to "focus and relax" while taking tests. Needless to say, both did very well in college.

Too often parents look at Kumon as some kind of remedial Band-aid. They put their children in and quit early. They don't understand Kumon as a tool for success.

– Laura Henry, mother, Sacramento, CA

How Can You Prove That it Works?

Talking to other Kumon parents is probably the best way to convince yourself of what Kumon can do for your own children.

However, quite a few parents want to see empirical evidence. They want to see test data and comparisons with control groups under carefully monitored conditions in order to fully accept the idea that Kumon really works.

There is nothing wrong with that kind of approach. Perhaps it is a matter of personal choice. Some people might say this method works better for choosing a car than a supplemental education system for your children, but there is absolutely nothing wrong with looking at data. The Kumon people keep mountains of data about how well students move through the different Kumon levels and where they have difficulties.

There have been studies done in North America with Kumon and there are more underway right now. One of the most rigorous studies was conducted in Tulsa, OK, and managed by staff from a famous school for gifted children called The University School (affiliated with the University of Tulsa). Interestingly, the study did not focus on students from The University School. Instead, it tested Kumon in a much more difficult setting, an inner-city elementary school, where students have few of the advantages of the children at The University School.

Dr. Patricia Hollingsworth, the Director of The University School, points out that this study was not sponsored by Kumon, but by the U.S. government. The Kumon Method was chosen because Dr. Hollingsworth is a firm believer in its effectiveness: she has been using it for over 12 years in her own school and was completely confident that it would be just as effective for economically disadvantaged children. "We have a Javits grant from the U.S. Department of Education," she explained, "part of which is to identify and nurture gifts and talents in young children. The problem is, how do you find out if you are gifted in math if you have never had a program where you can move along at your own pace? This is our third year in using Kumon in the Hawthorne school in northern Tulsa, and it has proven to be very effective... Children who have done it have shown good test results."

Two 8-month studies were conducted at Hawthorne, in 1999-2000 using second graders, and in 2000-2001 using third graders. In each study, two classrooms of students from the same school followed their normal course of math instruction, but one class also used Kumon as a supplement to their regular school math exercises, while the other class did not. All the students were tested before and after the study.

Was there any measurable difference in the group that did Kumon? Of course there was: tests showed that 100% of the 2nd graders who supplemented school math with Kumon increased their math skills. Among 3rd graders the number was 95%. The students were tested using a standardized test, the Iowa Test of Basic Skills. Two ITBS math sub-tests were used, Math Concepts and Math Problems. Just for comparison, a look at the average Math Concepts scores for the 2nd graders showed that children in the Kumon group had a mean score of 53.8, while those in the non-Kumon group scored 29.2. For Math Problems the numbers were: Kumon group—52.6, non-Kumon group—30.2.

Then, one year after the study finished, the former 3rd graders were tested again to see if they had retained anything from their studies more than a year ago. Dr. Hollingsworth again: "We found that the children who had Kumon in 3rd grade but not in 4th grade still tested better in 4th grade than their counterparts who didn't have Kumon. There was measurable retention over a year of not having Kumon."

The monitors of this study concluded, "The results reinforced the hypothesis that a supplemental mathematics curriculum such as the Kumon Method, which emphasizes repetition, speed, and accuracy in basic concepts, can greatly enhance math programs in economically disadvantaged schools." Dr. Hollingsworth summed it up this way: "We tested children who had done Kumon against a group of their peers that didn't, and of course the Kumon group greatly outperformed. Kumon is not a low-maintenance program, but the rewards of doing it are tremendous."

Another study, conducted by the Hawaii State Department of Education, ran for approximately 16 months beginning in early 1992. Nearly 200 elementary school students completed the entire pilot program, which focused only on mathematics. A summary of the study includes the following comments:

Fourth grade students in the Kumon program did

achieve significantly better than did students in the comparison group on all subtests of the SAT and on the geometry test. Seventy-nine (79) percent or more of the Kumon and non-Kumon teachers noticed improvement in the students' computational skills. Fifty-eight (58) percent of the Kumon teachers and 38 percent of the non-Kumon teachers noticed improvement in their study habits. Over 50 percent of all of the teachers recognized improvement in the students' concentration, in math and in their liking for mathematics. Compared with the non-Kumon students, significantly more Kumon students like mathematics, look forward to mathematics class, and find the mathematics class challenging. In addition, they do not find mathematics boring nor working with numbers upsetting.

Research conducted by Teachers College, Columbia University at a New York City elementary school found that "Kumon students at both primary and intermediate levels performed visibly better than matched peers on mathematics skills . . . and also had better completion times, and tended to attempt more items that were harder." (*A Summative Evaluation Report of the Kumon Supplemental Instructional Program*, M. Chatterji, Ph.D., et al, Teachers College, Columbia University, September, 2002.)

Yet another experiment was conducted in Ontario, Canada, starting in 2000. Kumon was selected for a pilot public/private sector educational project involving children in foster care. The six-month project included 68 children, almost two-thirds of whom were in grades 4-8 and roughly one-third of whom were in kindergarten. At the time of enrollment all the students completed a placement test, which helped to identify the ideal "comfortable starting point" for each child. The group reported spending an average of under 15 minutes per night on their homework assignments, which is not unusual for any Kumon students at these levels.

Half a year later (not long enough for students to derive the full benefit of Kumon study) they were re-tested with the same placement test as part of an evaluation of the program. Two-thirds of the students reported receiving higher grades since starting the program, and school report cards for that period bore that out: 71% of the students received improved grades in the school subject corresponding directly to their Kumon study. Moreover, in just this short period, the tests indicated significant improvements in speed (31% reduction in completion times) and accuracy (11% improvement in test scores). This initial evaluation showed that even in the short term, Kumon can be effective.

There is more and more evidence about Kumon—from medical and academic research, from field experiments with school groups, even from anecdotal evidence from teachers, parents and Instructors who see the results of Kumon right in front of their eyes. People all across the country will tell you: Kumon works.

I know it works, 'cause just a few weeks after my son started going to Kumon I saw his test scores jump. He started getting 100%, 100% every time. He always used to get a few mistakes, maybe 95%, but never 100. My girlfriend was saying, "Oh, I can teach my own son," but I said, "No, take him to Kumon. You will see the difference."

– Lesley Mafi, mother, Oakland, CA

Her scores on the standardized tests are incredibly good and her eagerness and ability to understand and apply math concepts have increased tremendously. I truly believe it is because of Kumon.

– Tony Nardo, father, Miami, FL

I understand the math, it's repetition and it's cut and dried, right or wrong, and I can see how that improves it, but I don't have a clue how the reading program has improved her comprehension, but it has. Her standard test scores have gone up. She went up 12 composite points in one year. I didn't put her in Kumon to improve her standardized test scores. I did it because she spent 4 and 5 and 6 hours on homework. She makes straight As, so her teachers always said; why do you want her to be better? and I said I don't; I want her to spend less time. She's going to make A's. I want her to be more efficient in her reading and understand it better. I would do anything to get her to do less homework. The reading comprehension has skyrocketed with Kumon.

– Terry Entwhistle, mother, St. Louis, MO

Chapter 9

Children with Special Needs

If you have followed Toru Kumon's basic philosophy of children outlined earlier, you already know the Kumon response to the "special needs" question: *Every* child has special needs. Gifted children have special needs and slow learners have special needs; physically challenged children and children with severe learning disabilities, foreign students who are trying to learn English and "ordinary" children doing average work in school—they all need special attention. Why? Because they are children, and they all need special attention in order to develop to their maximum potential. That is part of what Kumon is all about.

First, a word of caution. There are hundreds of stories about Kumon helping children with special needs and more seem to appear every week. Parents sometimes bring a child to Kumon specifically because they have heard one of these stories. These stories must spread by word of mouth. Kumon cannot in good conscience promote itself as a cure, treatment, or therapy for any kind of medical or psychological condition. The reason Kumon does not advertise or promote its successes in dealing with "special needs" children has to do with the sensitive nature of the problems involved. What is beneficial in one child's case may prove of no value in another. Kumon does not make any therapeutic claims or mislead parents into thinking of Kumon as a therapy or treatment.

Yet it is an undeniable fact that parents of many children with learning problems continue to report that Kumon has helped them. In March each year the Kumon organization in Japan holds a multi-day conference for special-needs students and their parents where new case studies and new instructional approaches are discussed. There are study sessions devoted to autism, Down's syndrome and various learning disabilities, among others. Over the years, many Japanese families have come to Kumon Centers for help, almost always through word-of-mouth recommendations, and many of their stories come out at these seminars. In fact, every year Kumon publishes a book which includes some of these stories as well as essays and statistics on the number of special-needs children registered in Kumon Centers throughout the country (just for your information, there were over 2,500 students with some kind of severe learning challenge registered in Kumon in Japan during the year 2000).

What is a learning disability? One legal definition says any child who is two years behind projected ability based on IQ has a learning disability. In practice, any child who is not able to learn in the same way or at the same rate as the majority of other children may be labeled as having a learning disability, whether that is actually the case or not. Schools generally refer children suspected of having a learning disability to a specialist or specialists who, after a thorough evaluation, can make a proper diagnosis. It is important to remember that just because a child does not achieve at the same academic level as his or her peers does *not* mean that the child has a learning disability. Moreover, there should be no social stigma attached to such disabilities. People like Albert Einstein and Thomas Edison were said to have had learning disabilities. That didn't stop them from excelling later in life.

In Japan, where Kumon has nearly a fifty-year history, there was a fifth grade Kumon student who was easily solving quadratic equations, finding square roots, and similar higher math functions. The child was formerly classified as autistic. Another child with a severe learning disability was solving simultaneous linear equations and reading at a high school level. She's in the second grade. A girl with Down's syndrome began doing Kumon at the age of six, and by ninth grade she was doing high school-level math. A Center for severely disabled children which introduced the Kumon Method reports that after children began learning Kumon they became more energetic, more willing to do their school homework, ate more, and showed better growth patterns. One of the Center's staff members, whose own child was studying three levels beyond her school grade level, said she wondered why Kumon hadn't told her earlier about the merits of the program for learning disabled children. This feeling seems to be growing, as more parents of children with special needs discover the special merits of doing Kumon.

Not only in Japan, but all across North America, Europe, Asia and in every country where Kumon is taught, there are similar reports of dramatic successes. Many of these are tremendous, heart-warming stories, some even more inspiring than those just mentioned. This naturally makes parents want to extol the virtues of the Kumon program as a panacea for physically and emotionally challenged children, for learning disabilities of all types, and much more. However, as we noted just a moment ago, Kumon cannot make such claims itself.

What the Kumon organization can say, because they have a wealth of data to back it up, is that the combination of time, patience, and long hours of hard work by learning-challenged children, as well as by supportive parents and dedicated Instructors can often lead to significant improvements in children with special needs. Time and again Kumon Instructors have seen a young child prove medical "experts" wrong and demonstrate Toru Kumon's first principle: none of us knows the true potential of any child in its formative years. As long as we encourage the child to keep trying, there is no definable limit to how far he or she can go, regardless of what we may perceive as a "disability."

Just as an example, I remember vividly a visit to a New York area Kumon Center some time ago. There I met a very bright, talkative child named Danny whose Instructor told me that he was one of the most accomplished students in her Center. Danny seemed to be just another one of those Kumon children who are destined for success. After he went into the next room to study, I met his mother, who told me that he wasn't always like that, and in fact his progress had been quite impressive.

> Danny is dyslexic. We took him to see a number of specialists and all of them told us essentially the same thing: he would most likely never be able to function the way 'normal' children do, that his reading and writing would always be affected, and so on. My husband and I tried several specialists, we put him in three different schools, and frankly we began to think that maybe the doctors were right. Then I heard from the mother of one of his friends about Kumon. Danny's math scores were pretty bad, so we thought we'd give it a try.
>
> He started with the very lowest levels where they make you draw numbers again and again. At first he drew all his numbers backwards, just as he always had. But as he repeated the homework again and again he began to change. Little by little his motor control improved. First he started drawing his numbers correctly, and then as he continued to practice, they became perfect. I mean absolutely perfect, they look like they'd been printed. We were delighted. Then his math scores started to go up, then his concentration went up, and that pulled up his other grades as well... I don't know what to say. We spent over $35,000 trying various kinds of special help for Danny and nothing worked. Now we've been doing Kumon for a couple of years, which costs so little in comparison, and we think it's the best thing we've found.

In St. Louis I met a mother named Julie who told me her son is classified as severely to profoundly deaf. "They told us from age 4 that he was going to have a lot of trouble learning to read. For him to hear sounds and put them down on paper correctly would be a big, big challenge. So we were very concerned about how his reading would develop. We started Kumon before kindergarten and saw a big jump in achievement around first grade. We started with cards and simple sounds and it was like a game for him. I think it's really helped his reading. Now he loves to read, and that means he doesn't have to depend on his ears so much. He learns a lot of things by reading them, which is a big help... Now his teacher at school says he is better at spelling than most children with normal hearing... I think it has also helped his self-esteem. Even if he had a rough day at school he was always happy to go to Kumon, because he knew he was good at Kumon."

At the University of Monterrey in Monterrey, Mexico, over 40 young adults with various mental impairments use Kumon as part of a special training program to become more independent and better integrated with the community. One mentally retarded student commented that "I love working with Kumon because besides learning mathematics I become more confident." A research associate supervising the program said, "Kumon is the best way for them to realize that life is made of small steps."

From Tulsa comes this letter from another Kumon mom:

Hi, my name is Karen and my oldest son was born with Down's syndrome. When I first heard about Kumon, well, suffice it to say that I tend to be a very skeptical person. But there were a few ideas in the Kumon philosophy that I liked... [such as] Kumon is for all children, no matter what level they are at, [and how important it is to] build in small steps; just do a little every day.

When my son started Kumon just a few months ago, he was able to count to 10—a skill he had been working on since kindergarten. He's in second grade now. In just a few weeks, he was able to count to 30. That may not seem like much, but for him it was a major accomplishment. He had basically tripled his knowledge of math. We were both *thrilled*!

He is continuing to make progress. Kumon is not only

teaching him math skills, but also fine motor skills and independent study. He does his homework by himself and then we check it. Although he is not always thrilled to do his homework, he says he loves Kumon. I think that's because when he's done he feels that he's accomplished something. What better gift to give a child of any ability level than the sense of pride and accomplishment.

Yash Mittal was born with Williams syndrome, a neuro-behavioral disorder that limits his IQ to 60. In spite of these challenges, his parents are determined to see him succeed in a regular school environment. They turned to Kumon for help. "I can surely say that Kumon has played a big role in his development," his father told me. Yash began Kumon as a 6 year old. Eight years later he is doing multiplication and division in Kumon Math and analyzing short passages in Kumon Reading. "He needs five to six repetitions but ultimately can perform and is able to comprehend. The key for any student, especially special needs students, is to be persistent, and give them confidence and encouragement. Yash is working very well because he can see the success and do the worksheets independently which is the motivating factor for him."

A mother in Miami told me her young son was diagnosed with ADD and put on Ritalin. He had a lot of problems in school, so she tried another school. No improvement. She put him in Kumon. His grades went up, his Ritalin medication went down, he got on the school Honor Roll and won 8 awards in math and reading. This was one happy mom. "He used to count on his fingers; now he does fraction problems in his head," she said proudly. The boy was beaming: "I was doing a math project at school, and I was doing division problems in my head in just a few seconds. People said I had magic!"

Or one of my favorites, another mother I met in the greater St. Louis area, Mrs. Drummer:

Randall is a very hyper child. He's very wiggly; at school he could never concentrate, so he never could finish his projects. He got distracted at any little thing, and it was hard for him to sit still and do anything.

Not only that, but he was always distracting other people. His kindergarten teacher wanted to put him on Ritalin. I said, 'No way.' I started looking for a tutor but another teacher said we should try Kumon instead. I said, 'What's a Kumon?' The Instructor explained that this is not a short-term solution and if we're looking for a tutor this is not the place. I liked that long-term approach, so we decided to try it. Randall started Kumon in first grade and has been doing it a little over a year. When we started at the Center, the Instructor was always saying, 'Randall . . . come sit down. Randall, please!. . .' It was a challenge, believe me. Now he comes in to the Center, he sits down, concentrates, and does his work. At home I just say, 'It's time.' And he sits down and does it, and when he's finished he says, 'It's done. Is there anything else you want me to do?' Sometimes he will just go and do his Kumon homework on his own without me saying anything. He didn't used to have that kind of initiative before. I finally decided to take him out of school, home-school him, but keep him in Kumon. . . .

He had an especially hard time reading and focusing. He would cry and kick and scream because he really couldn't read a lot of words and he was embarrassed. He could read a word and tell you what it was, but the next time he saw the same word he couldn't recognize it for some reason. The repetition in Kumon really helped. Now he loves to read. He can read things confidently and remembers what he reads. If you ask him to read something now he's happy. He wants to read. He reads stories to me sometimes. Every day I make him read something to me, I say, 'I used to read to you a lot when you were little, now it's your turn to read to me.' He sleeps with his books now.

He's come a long way, a very long way. In the past, when he reached hard spots he didn't know how to work through it, how to overcome it, but Kumon has taught him that it might be hard but if you keep working at it you will succeed. So now when he hits hard spots he says to himself, 'I know I can overcome this; I did it before, I know I'll get it this time.' He knows he's an achiever. Kumon has helped to build his self-esteem. It's been—I would have to call it a miracle, in both math and reading.

Kerri Niday, a mother in a suburb of San Francisco, put it this way:

Kumon is really good for children with learning disabilities. My daughter has a motor-visual disability. They told me that she needs a lot of repetition to move things from short-term to long-term memory. Kumon was the only thing that seemed to do that. And we've definitely noticed an improvement, in both my children, in fact. You look at 'special ed' programs in the schools. They don't do anything. They modify, they cut back on what the children do. That's just a big step backwards. Children with learning disabilities need *more*, not less. Not more volume, of course, but more repetition, because that's what gets it into their heads. But the schools always want to cut it down, make it simpler, not expect so much of these children. Look, my daughter has a learning disability but she also has a normal IQ. I don't want her to be babied. By putting her in Kumon she goes way ahead of the other children, and pretty soon the school says she doesn't need to be in special ed anymore.

We could go on and on. I have talked to many parents of children with Down's syndrome and a variety of other challenges. In every case, parents reported that after a year or so in Kumon they saw changes they did not believe possible. Sometimes small things at first, but always building towards the kind of real, heartwarming progress that too many parents are afraid to hope for any more. Nor are these merely academic accomplishments. Some parents reported that their children suddenly learned to dress themselves, and that motor skills, activity levels, and even appetites improved.

Needless to say, none of these things happens overnight.

Educational progress with almost any child requires time and patience on the part of the parent, and with a special needs child it requires much more. However, if you truly believe in your child's potential just as Kumon does, your faith will inevitably be communicated to your child. If the parent is supportive, and the study materials are used properly, the child will discover that he or she can study, learn, and progress beyond anyone's expectations. As the results become apparent little by little, the child discovers a greater sense of self-esteem. This alone can lead to more satisfactory performance in other areas as well.

After decades of evidence with thousands and thousands of children, there is good reason to believe that the appropriate use of Kumon materials in a patient, supportive manner will lead to an improvement in students' academic ability and often in other forms of physical and emotional development as well. The bottom line is that Kumon can be a useful tool in working with children who present special challenges. Like any approach, however, it requires extra time and attention from both the parents and the Instructor. If your child needs special attention, call the nearest Center and talk about it with your local Instructor. Find out if there are other such children in the Center and how the local Instructor would recommend that you plan to climb the Kumon path to knowledge.

I have met so many parents who say their local school informed them that their child is having learning problems and perhaps the child needs therapy. The parents are very worried that their child will have no hope for a bright future. These kinds of parents are very communicative with me about their children, and they tell me that their children are changing with Kumon. With the Kumon Method children learn to value themselves and to feel confident and secure. The parents tell me that it does not matter if the child is working with materials that are below grade level—they can see that their children are no longer afraid of doing school work and are feeling more positive about learning and studying in all their subjects.

– Ana Teresa de Jesús Velásquez Centeno,
Kumon Instructor, México City, Mexico

Chapter 10

You Can't Start Too Early!

Here is a scene that is re-enacted week after week across North America: A mother visits a local Kumon Center, perhaps to pick up her son or daughter who has just completed today's work, and asks to speak to the Instructor. What about the child's 5-year-old younger brother or sister? How soon should they think about enrolling the little one in Kumon? And many a Kumon Instructor has the same reply: "What are you waiting for?"

I suspect that if Toru Kumon could have re-designed the world he would have made sure that every child on the planet began some kind of structured education from about the age of six months. Remember that the Kumon philosophy centers not on math or reading, but on the child, on the potential of every child to develop further and faster than adults imagine. Unlike the body, which takes 15 years to grow to roughly 80% of its adult size, the brain is close to its full size when the child is still in kindergarten. Yet because the body is small and fragile, some assume the child's mind is likewise, and try to "protect" it from too much information. It is a fact that even very young children can acquire enormous amounts of information, such as math basics or vocabulary, with no apparent effort. The real problem is not their ability, which is almost limitless, but their attention span. For this reason, formal education can start early but it must be limited to short doses, 5-10 minutes here and 10-15 minutes there. Once the child discovers the pleasure of drawing letters and numbers (together with friends of the same age and a caring Instructor), the door is open and the child will likely astonish you with how fast he or she learns.

This is not some abstract theory proposed by educational psychologists, but rather, the result of decades of instruction with tens of thousands of children. Although no comparative statistics are available, it is a pretty safe bet that Kumon worldwide has collected more data on the formative years of children than any research study, public or private. In other words, Kumon knows at least as well as (and perhaps better than) most scholars the true capacity of young minds to absorb, understand and retain information.

This vast experience with very young minds did not come quickly. In the early years, even Toru Kumon himself did not understand the full potential of the young mind. It is only through time and the results of so many children studying in Kumon Centers around the world that the truth has become apparent. For example, it took 19 years from the founding of the Kumon Institute of Education in Japan before a pre-school student was able to solve equations. Equations are introduced in the Japanese system in the 7th grade, and in the U.S. usually a bit later. For an elementary school child to be able to handle equations easily is quite a feat, but for a pre-school child to do so seems amazing. At least it did in 1977 when two pre-schoolers in Kumon advanced to the point where they were working with equations. Even then the younger of the two was six years old. By 1988 the youngest student working with equations was 26 months old, and just four years later over 600 pre-school children had reached this same level.

These children are not geniuses. They are perfectly normal children who started Kumon early and got caught up in the joy of learning at their own pace and progressing through the different levels. Simply put, children absorb information if it is presented well; they respond to praise; and they naturally want to do more of what they are good at. The result is not genius children, but children who can study far ahead of their grade level and who exhibit a sense of self-confidence that lasts throughout their school careers. One survey showed that all pre-schoolers who learn to do equations also develop a very high reading ability. Kumon is confident that at least 90% of the children who begin their studies at the pre-school age will become outstanding all-around students.

Speaking of reading, in Japan, many pre-schoolers learn to read via Kumon (and learning to read the 94 phonetic alphabet characters plus several hundred basic Chinese characters is a lot more difficult than learning to read the English alphabet). Despite the intricacy of the Japanese language, there are students who learn to read all the basic characters by the age of two. Currently, Kumon in Japan expects a two-year-old child to learn to read in roughly six months of simple daily study. Parents of two- and three-year-olds say their children read for entertainment rather than watching TV. This means that, not only will the child's vocabulary, spelling ability, and comprehension skills increase dramatically, but also the child's intelligence and curiosity will be stimulated by the world of books.

Yes, I'm talking about two- and three-year-olds.

Kumon is not saying that you should expect your pre-schooler to be doing high school-level math, or that you should push your child to become a "super child." What they are saying is that even very young children have an amazing potential to learn and to advance if presented with good materials in a supportive environment. The keys are *patience*, *practice* and *praise*. Kumon Instructors hope that in the not-too-distant future stories of children doing higher-level math or reading junior-high-level books at an early age will not be seen as strange. That will mean that people are beginning to accept the fact that ordinary children already *are* super children.

"They are just like flowers," one Instructor said to me, "You give them water and sunshine and watch them blossom. They never fail to amaze you."

We started Isabelle in Kumon at 2 years and 9 months. Now I wish we had started even earlier.

– Judy Wong, mother, Long Island, NY

At my daughter's fifth birthday party, she was less interested in her presents than in reading what people had written in her birthday cards. All the other parents were stunned. They asked me, "How is that possible?" and I said, "Well, this is Kumon." She has really developed wonderfully as a reader, and she enjoys reading very much. When she is bad, I tell her that her punishment is she can't read a book that day.

– Fairosa Rajpurkar, mother, Maryland Heights, MO

We started Alex in Kumon in grade one for him to develop an interest in math and discipline for studying and doing homework from an early age.

– Vivian Wan, mother, AL, Canada

Skills and Self-confidence

There are plenty of good reasons to start your children in Kumon early. Probably the best one is that they learn all the fundamentals of any subject while it is still easy and painless to do so. A good example is Roger Hong, whom I met in Cambridge, MA, where he is a student at Harvard. Roger started Kumon at five years old. He told me, "I can't even remember starting Kumon. All I remember is that I thought it was fun. My parents were pretty busy working, so I did my homework by myself. Because I started by drawing lines, it was pretty easy and I didn't need any help. By the time it got harder, I had already gotten into the routine of doing it."

Another important point is building self-confidence before children ever go off to school. A mother in California told me about her daughter: "Christina wanted to read from an early age. I tried to work with her to help her to read, but whatever I was doing just wasn't doing the trick. Then I put her in the Kumon Reading program and within a month or so she was reading. The key is to start them young. Because Christina started early, she knew how to read before she entered kindergarten, and that gave her tremendous self-confidence."

Does that self-confidence carry over as the years go by and the child advances through grade levels in school? Of course, she said. "Christina comes home and says, 'Oh, they had some story in school today but I already read it in Kumon.' She's a happy little girl."

It is also worth remembering that getting started in Kumon is nothing like starting your child in classroom-style rote learning. Not only is it completely individualized, but it is designed to be fun. There are dozens of useful tools for teaching toddlers these days—music, jigsaw puzzles, tracing games, alphabet cards, etc.—and Kumon takes advantage of them. For example, jigsaw puzzles are especially useful for toddlers because they develop both manual dexterity and the ability to concentrate. Therefore, Kumon created its own series of jigsaw puzzles just in the way you would expect—a stepped progression of 24 levels designed to take the child from very simple (2-piece) constructions to very complex (330-piece) patterns. The puzzles are so popular that they have been made commercially available in Japan and sell very well. It's easy to see why. My older son was playing with Kumon puzzles (a present from his grandma) long before I knew anything about Kumon. When he was very young he started with the simplest ones, learned to do them correctly, and when he could do them quickly and easily he let Mom and Dad know that he didn't find them challenging any more and he wanted new ones. So we bought him the next puzzle in the progression, he mastered that, then we bought him the next, and so on. In the process we both learned that in a fundamental way speed and accuracy are sure signs that a child has mastered one level and is ready for the next.

Based on information obtained from its international network of Instructors, Kumon is still developing new materials to stimulate young minds. More and more parents are realizing that there is no reason to hold their children back. That small, fragile body holds an active, inquisitive mind. It will absorb almost anything presented to it, including mathematics and languages. If your child is old enough to hold a pencil, he or she is old enough to start Kumon and begin to reap the benefits.

My daughter started Kumon at age three. A lot of people thought I was crazy because Morgan was so young, and now I find that Kumon works with lots of children younger than she was. I didn't know where it would lead, but I thought 'Lets give it a try.' And now I'm so glad we did it. It's so organized, you're not missing anything. A lot of people say, 'I can teach my child to read' or 'I can teach my child arithmetic,' but you could easily be missing something important. You're just going on instinct. With Kumon, you know they're going to hit every step in the right order because someone's thought about it already.

– Laura Henry, mother, Sacramento, CA

So I put him in Kumon when he had just turned 4. I asked our Instructor 'Is he too young?' and she said, 'Not at all. Start him with math and then we'll move on to reading. Don't be worried if he doesn't seem to get things; everything will be all right.' And it was. We started with math and then reading about six months later.

– Bonnie Farias, mother, Danville, CA

I met a little 3-year-old at my Center, and when I asked if she could write her name, she said, "Yes, I can." But when I gave her a paper and pencil, she wrote the number 1610 and proudly announced that it was her name. I was very amused, and thought what a confident little girl she is and how much she would benefit from the direction and guidance Kumon can offer. Now little Daniela is one of my best students. She is already adding +1 and +2 [to other numbers—a basic Kumon exercise]. She proudly says, "The answers just show up in my head." I have seen the benefits of Kumon build upon her enthusiasm and desire to learn.

**– Ana Teresa de Jesús Velásquez Centeno,
Kumon Instructor, México City, Mexico**

Chapter 11

A Message to North American Parents
from Chairman Hiroshi Kumon

Kumon:
An International
Phenomenon

In the mid-1950s, when my father first began to create the method that would later bear his name, he knew that this student-centered approach to learning was the best way to help young minds to develop. He truly believed that a child's mind is the most wondrous thing in the world, and so he wanted his ideas to spread beyond his own home. From this first seed the Kumon Institute of Education was born.

Not only was his dream realized in the city where he first conceived it, but in time it spread across an entire nation, and then outwards, across the globe. In fact, the Kumon system has grown steadily from its humble roots in my father's house to become the single most successful private educational program in the world.

There are many reasons for this success. Of course, the most important is that Toru Kumon's approach was intuitively right to begin with. There was a vast pent-up demand—not only in Japan, but in other countries as well—for a carefully designed system that could help children reveal their innate potential for learning rather than simply stuffing their heads full of facts. This system, combined with excellent study materials, and legions of dedicated, carefully trained Instructors, was all that was needed to turn Kumon into an international phenomenon. Now, with the proven success of millions of students, and many millions of satisfied parents who can discuss the virtues of the Kumon Method with their friends, our continued growth is assured.

I am especially pleased to see Kumon growing so quickly in North America. I think that North American parents do not realize how lucky they are to live in such a unique environment. Your children have access to some of the finest educational resources in the world. Not only are there countless good schools with well-stocked libraries, computers and other advanced facilities that are the envy of other countries, but your children are also exposed to a rich palette of sports, music, art, and other cultural activities, both in school and outside. In many cases, they have every opportunity imaginable to grow and realize their full potential.

Kumon was created to help that process. Regardless of what kind of school environment is available, Kumon can help a child to grow, both in terms of academic achievement and personal character. Kumon, as most of you know, not only builds a solid foundation of academic discipline, but also builds study skills, self-confidence, and self-esteem. I know that these qualities are important to North American parents because every month I see how many thousands of you have enrolled your own children to start on the Kumon path.

From what I read and what I hear in my travels, I think that North American parents are increasingly interested in the kind of back-to-basics approach that Kumon embodies and in the dramatic results it can provide. As this book points out, Kumon is not a "quick fix," nor will it help those who cannot study just a little bit every day. However, for those parents and children who are able to make a small daily commitment the results can be startling.

It may sound strange coming from the founder's son, but in spite of its origins I don't think of Kumon as "Japanese" in any real sense. Kumon is no more a Japanese system than it is an American system or a French system or any other kind of system. Kumon is a *universally applicable* method to help students to maximize their learning achievement regardless of age, race, cultural background or apparent ability. Kumon is designed for only one purpose—to serve its students, whoever and wherever they may be. Although for historical reasons Kumon happened to start in Japan, it is now growing very rapidly in North America, an area with a much larger population than Japan. It is only a matter of time before the total Kumon enrollment in North America will surpass that in Japan. Will that make Kumon an "American system"? Not at all. Kumon has no cultural identity. It is an international movement. Perhaps someday the European enrollment will be the largest in the world. What difference will that make? The only thing that matters to me is that the greatest number of children worldwide have an opportunity to develop their vast potential to learn. A better educated world is our best hope for lasting peace and prosperity.

Nothing could please me more than to think that the borderless learning system called Kumon is helping children around the world to get the most from their education, to grow and develop and become mature, responsible global citizens. This is the ultimate dream behind Kumon. It was my father's dream, and it is my dream, too.

Hiroshi Kumon
Osaka, Japan
Spring 2002

Chapter 12
A Message from Toru Kumon,
Founder of the Kumon Institute of Education

The Kumon Method in North America

Parents frequently ask me, "What is the most important thing to remember in teaching my children?" I always reply with a question: How much confidence do you have in your children's potential? It is vitally important that we do not set artificial limits on what children are capable of doing. I could give dozens of examples, but the first one that comes to mind is that of a mentally handicapped girl who recently sat for a Japanese high school entrance exam (a very difficult test for any student). She was a good Kumon student and worked very hard at her studies, so we had no doubt that she would succeed. But the school officials were astounded. Clearly, because they knew of her learning disability, they had developed false preconceptions about the limits of this girl's abilities.

My point is that children must be given every opportunity to succeed. It is a terrible shame for parents to give up on any child's abilities before he or she has had a real chance to grow. This is why I say that it is crucial for both parents and children to have a positive, "Let's try!" attitude. If you foster this attitude in your own children, you will be amazed at what they can do. I firmly believe that this is our most important duty as parents.

Then why do we here at Kumon promote mathematics?

Most people who have heard of the Kumon Method know that it helps children to do mathematical calculations faster than they could before. But the main objective of the Kumon Method is something more general: to give students the ability to study ahead of their grade level in school. When students study two or three years ahead of their grade level, they will not only master mathematics, but will also gradually learn how to study any subject on their own. In my experience, such children tend to develop certain common traits regardless of their backgrounds: a tremendous natural curiosity, self-confidence, perseverance, and the ability to concentrate. These traits help children to develop not only their mathematical abilities, but their athletic and artistic abilities as well. Because of this, I believe that the skills and habits that the Kumon Method helps to build can improve a child's life in many ways.

At last count, more than 1.6 million children in Japan and 350,000 children in 28 countries around the world were studying with the Kumon Educational Method. I am especially pleased to see the Kumon Method spreading so quickly in North America because your society emphasizes making the most of individual abilities. In many schools there are systems for advanced students to skip grades, and there are special classes for gifted children. This tells me that Americans and Canadians also believe in the importance of developing children's abilities, regardless of their grade level.

On the other hand, there are still relatively few systems and institutions to help children whose scholastic abilities are below average. I sincerely hope that all children, whatever their level of scholastic ability, will have a chance to study with the Kumon Method because we consider it our mission to bring out the hidden potential in each and every child.

As the benefits of the Kumon Method become better

known, it will continue to grow, to 2 million, 3 million, and perhaps beyond. I look forward to the day when these millions of children—self-disciplined, self-motivated, and self-confident—will reward our faith in them by making their own contributions to society.

Toru Kumon
Osaka, Japan
October 1993

Appendix I

The Kumon Method of Education Throughout the World

The Number of Kumon Students as of September 2002

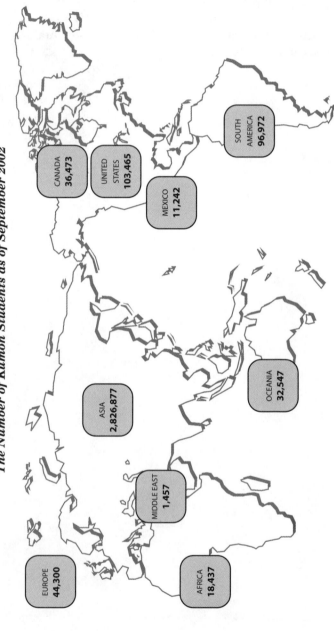

CANADA
36,473

UNITED STATES
103,465

MEXICO
11,242

SOUTH AMERICA
96,972

EUROPE
44,300

AFRICA
18,437

MIDDLE EAST
1,457

ASIA
2,826,877

OCEANIA
32,547

Appendix II

Kumon's
Spectacular Growth

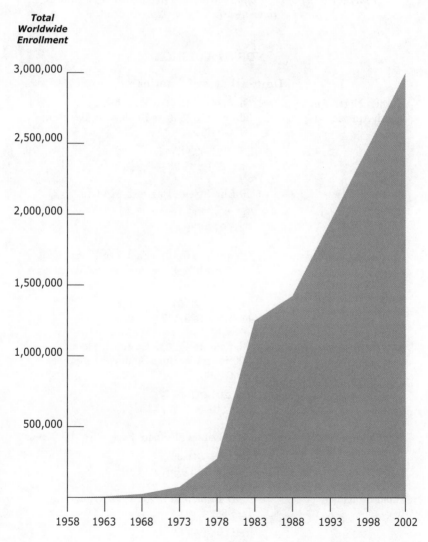

Data: Kumon Institute of Education 09/02

Appendix III

Kumon Offices

For those parents who would like to learn more about Kumon,
I include a list of their offices to contact for further information,
or visit their website at www.kumon.com

NORTH AMERICA

United States of America

Kumon North America, Inc. North America HQ	Glenpointe Centre East, 5th Floor, 300 Frank W. Burr Boulevard, Teaneck, NJ 07666
	Tel: 201-928-0444 Fax: 201-928-0044
Boston Office	10 Elm Street, Danvers, MA 01923
	Tel: 978-739-4227 Fax: 978-739-4727
New Jersey Office	Glenpointe Centre East, 5th Floor, 300 Frank W. Burr Boulevard, Teaneck, NJ 07666
	Tel: 201-928-0777 Fax: 201-928-1777
New York Office	Glenpointe Centre East, 5th Floor, 300 Frank W. Burr Boulevard, Teaneck, NJ 07666
	Tel: 201-928-0777 Fax: 201-928-1777
Washington, D.C. Office	5210 Randolph Road, Rockville, MD 20852
	Tel: 301-231-6977 Fax: 301-231-6979
Honolulu Office	1357 Kapiolani Blvd., #1520 Honolulu, HI 96814
	Tel: 808-949-6284 Fax: 808-949-7323

Los Angeles Office	990 W. 190th Street, #200, Torrance, CA 90502 Tel: 310-225-2968 Fax: 310-323-6640
San Fernando Valley Office	990 W. 190th Street, #200, Torrance, CA 90502 Tel: 310-225-2968 Fax: 310-323-6640
Orange County Office	15707 Rockfield Boulevard, Suite 150, Irvine, CA 92618 Tel: 949-598-7222 Fax: 949-598-7220
Phoenix Office	4710 E. Elwood Street, #15, Phoenix, AZ 85040 Tel: 480-784-2992 Fax: 480-784-1677
San Francisco Office	111 Anza Blvd., #100, Burlingame, CA 94010 Tel: 650-347-8818 Fax: 650-347-8909
Seattle Office	10624 N. E. 37th Circle, Kirkland, WA 98033 Tel: 425-828-6284 Fax: 425-822-6769
Chicago Office	Two Continental Towers, #103, 1701 Golf Road, Rolling Meadows, IL 60008 Tel: 847-640-2354 Fax: 847-640-3067
Cincinnati Office	Prospect Square, 9708 Kenwood Road, Blue Ash, OH 45242 Tel: 513-745-0004 Fax: 513-745-9977
Detroit Office	29480 Woodward Avenue, Royal Oak, MI 48073 Tel: 248-541-7780 Fax: 248-541-7720

Every Child An Achiever

St. Louis Office	2045 Dorsett Village, Maryland Hts., MO 63043 Tel: 314-576-2600 Fax: 314-576-6600
Atlanta Office	3950 Shackleford Road, Suite 325, Duluth, GA 30096 Tel: 678-244-6284 Fax: 678-244-6285
Dallas Office	2120 E. Southlake Blvd., Suite A, Southlake, TX 76092 Tel: 817-329-6284 Fax: 817-421-1252
Houston Office	19901 Kingsland Blvd., Suites A & B, Houston, TX 77094 Tel: 281-599-3299 Fax: 281-599-3201
Florida Office	801 South University Drive, Suite 101-B, Plantation, FL 33324 Tel: 954-370-1057 Fax: 954-370-6390

Kumon Canada Inc.

Kumon Canada HQ	344 Consumers Road, North York, ON M2J 1P8 Tel: 416-490-1434 Fax: 416-490-1694
Vancouver Office	Metrotower 2, 1203-4720 Kingsway, Burnaby, BC V5H 4N2 Tel: 604-454-1001 Fax: 604-454-1002
Calgary Office	1503 19th Street N. W., Calgary, AB T2N 2K2 Tel: 403-244-0157 Fax: 403-244-0857

Toronto West Office	1140 Burnhamthorpe Road West, Suite 201, Mississauga, ON L5C 4E9
	Tel: 905-848-9148
	Fax: 905-848-9149
Toronto East Office	344 Consumers Road, North York, ON M2J 1P8
	Tel: 416-490-1434
	Fax: 416-490-1694
Montreal Office	1240 Beaumont Avenue, Suite 140, Mount-Royal, PQ H3P 3E5
	Tel: 514-733-3889
	Fax: 514-733-2700

Kumon Instituto de Educación, S. A. de C. V.

Mexico City Office	Arquímedes No. 130, Piso 7, Col. Polanco, Mexico, D.F., C. P. 11560
	Tel: 55-5281-2346
	Fax: 55-5281-3180

SOUTH AMERICA

Kumon Instituto de Educação, S/C Ltda.

South America HQ	Rua Tomás Carvalhal, 686, Paraíso, CEP 04006-002, São Paulo, SP., BRASIL
	Tel: 11-3059-3700
	Fax: 11-3884-6051
São Paulo Office	Rua Tomás Carvalhal, 686, Paraíso, CEP 04006-002, São Paulo, SP., BRASIL
	Tel: 11-3059-3711
	Fax: 11-3887-3038

Kumon Instituto de Educación de Chile Limitada

Santiago Office	Avenida Holanda 160, Providencia, Santiago
	Tel: 2-234-9288
	Fax: 2-234-9311

Kumon Instituto de Educación de Argentina S. R. L.

Buenos Aires Office   Mariscal Antonio J. de Sucre 2560,
Capital Federal, 1428

Tel: 11-4781-7555
Fax: 11-4781-0482

ASIA and OCEANIA

Japan

KUMON Headquarters   Kumon Institute of Education
5-6-6 Nishinakajima,
Yodogawa-ku, Osaka 532

Tel: 06-838-2619
Fax: 06-838-2705

Kumon Asia & Oceania Pte. Ltd.

Asia & Oceania HQ   9 Raffles Place #18-20/21 Republic Plaza II,
048619 SINGAPORE

Tel: 6232-5825
Fax: 6232-5833

Singapore Office   9 Raffles Place #18-20/21 Republic Plaza II,
048619 SINGAPORE

Tel: 6232-5855
Fax: 6232-5822

Kumon Asia & Oceania Pte. Ltd.

Kuala Lumpur Office   1209 A, 11th Floor, Kelana Parkview Tower,
No. 1, Jalan SS6/2, Kelana Jaya,
47301 Petaling Jaya, Selangor, MALAYSIA

Tel: 03-7806-1870
Fax: 03-7806-1876

Kumon Thailand Co., Ltd.

Bangkok Office   19/F B West 2, 18 SCB Park Plaza,
Ratchadapisek Rd., Ladyao, Jatuchak,
BKK 10900

Tel: 02-937-6036
Fax: 02-937-6037

Kumon Philippines, Inc.

Manila Office
19th Floor, Philamlife Tower,
8767 Paseo de Roxas Makati, Metro Manila

Tel: 02-885-0226
Fax: 02-885-0251

PT KIE INDONESIA

Jakarta Office
Setiabudi 2 Building, 3A Floor,
JL. H.R. Rasuna Said, Kuningan,
Jakarta 12920

Tel: 021-520-1051
Fax: 021-525-5981

Surabaya Office
Gedung Bumi Mandiri 8th Floor, JL Jendral
Basuki Rachmat 129-137, Surabaya 60271

Tel: 031-547-9540
Fax: 031-547-9539

Shanghai Kumon Educational Software Co., Ltd.

Shanghai Office
Room 2106-2108, Aetna Tower, 107 Zun Yi
Road, Shanghai, CHINA 200051

Tel: 021-6237-5866
Fax: 021-6237-5107

Kumon Hong Kong Co., Ltd.

Hong Kong Office
Unit 4301, 43F, Cosco Tower,
183 Queen's Road Central, HONG KONG

Tel: 2890-6533
Fax: 2894-8285

Tsuen Wan Office
Unit 1701-03, City Landmark 1, 68 Chung
On Street, Tsuen Wan, N.T., HONG KONG

Tel: 2940-6166
Fax: 2940-7377

Kumon Australia Pty Ltd.

Sydney Office Level 3, 22 Atchison Street,
St. Leonards, NSW 2065

Tel: 02-9467-2200
Fax: 02-9438-1848

Melbourne Office Level 3, 40 Albert Road,
South Melbourne, VIC 3025

Tel: 03-9696-1566
Fax: 03-9696-2619

Brisbane Office Ground Floor, 47 Warner Street,
Fortitude Valley, QLD 4006

Tel: 07-3257-3590
Fax: 07-3257-3596

Perth Office Level 9, 251 Adelaide Terrace,
Perth, WA 6000

Tel: 08-9325-8900
Fax: 08-9325-8909

Adelaide Office Level 1, 289 Flindars Street,
Adelaide, SA 5000

Tel: 08-8232-8500
Fax: 08-8823-8511

EUROPE & AFRICA

Kumon Educational U.K. Co., Ltd.

Europe & Africa HQ 5th Floor, The Grange, 100 High Street,
Southgate, London N14 6BN

Tel: 020-8447-9010
Fax: 020-8447-9030

London Office 5th Floor, The Grange, 100 High Street,
Southgate, London N14 6BN

Tel: 020-8447-9010
Fax: 020-8447-9030

Manchester Office Ground Floor, Landmark House,
Station Road, Cheadle Hulme, SK8 7GE

Tel: 0161-488-4988
Fax: 0161-488-4980

Bristol Office
Cambridge House, 34 Cambridge Crescent,
Westbury on Trym, Bristol BS9 3QG
Tel: 0117-962-8777
Fax: 0117-962-8666

Kumon Deutschland GmbH

Düsseldorf Office
Hansaallee 201, 40549 Düsseldorf,
GERMANY
Tel: 0211-594077
Fax: 0211-594027

Kumon Instituto de Educación de España, S.A.

Madrid Office
Bravo Murillo, 377 Primera Planta Oficina
C, 28020 Madrid, SPAIN
Tel: 91-323-1053
Fax: 91-315-1579

Kumon Education South Africa (PTY) Ltd.

Johannesburg Office
1 Ninth St., Houghton 2198, P.O. Box 1417,
Houghton 2041, Johannesburg
Tel: 011-788-4303
Fax: 011-788-4327

Cape Town Office
7 Waverley Studio, Waverley Business Park,
Mowbray, Cape Town 7700
Tel: 021-448-9991
Fax: 021-448-9996

Durban Office
Suite 16, GRANADA 16 Chartwell Drive,
Umhlanga Rocks 4320
Tel: 031-561-5024
Fax: 031-561-5742

LIAISON OFFICE

Kumon Institute of Education, Co., Ltd.

Seoul Office   5F., Joonghoo Bldg., 61-21, Taepyongro 1-ga,
Jung-gu 100-101, Seoul, KOREA

Tel: 02-739-8511
Fax: 02-739-8512

LICENSED AGENT

Kumon Cultural Enterprise Co., Ltd.

Taipei Office   Chi Kuang Center for Banking &
Commerce, 5FL., No. 48, Min Chuan West
Road, 104, Taipei, TAIWAN, R.O.C

Tel: 02-2543-2391
Fax: 02-2541-4549

*For information on Kumon Centers in the following countries,
please contact the corresponding office:*

Austria	Düsseldorf Office
France	Düsseldorf Office
Italy	Düsseldorf Office
Hungary	Düsseldorf Office
Switzerland	Düsseldorf Office
Colombia	São Paulo Office
Peru	São Paulo Office
All Other Countries	Osaka Headquarters